The Fight-Free Marriage

THE FIGHT-FREE MARRIAGE

The Conflict Without Casualty Strategy to a Satisfying Marriage

TOM ANASTASI

THOMAS NELSON PUBLISHERS
NASHVILLE • ATLANTA • LONDON • VANCOUVER

Published in Nashville, Tennessee, by Thomas Nelson, Inc., Publishers, and distributed in Canada by Word Communications, Ltd., Richmond, British Columbia, and in the United Kingdom by Word (UK), Ltd., Milton Keynes, England.

Scripture quotations noted are from THE NEW KING JAMES VERSION. Copyright © 1979, 1980, 1982, 1990 Thomas Nelson, Inc., Publishers.

Scripture quotations noted RSV are from the REVISED STANDARD VERSION of the Bible. Copyright © 1946, 1952, 1971, 1973 by the Division of Christian Education of the National Council of the Churches of Christ in the U.S.A. Used by permission.

Conflict Without Casualty™ is a trademark of Sales & Negotiation Training Company.

Library of Congress Cataloging-in-Publication Data

Anastasi, Thomas E.
    The fight-free marriage : the conflict without casualty strategy to a satisfying marriage / Tom Anastasi.
      p. cm.
    Includes bibliographical references.
    ISBN 0-7852-7937-7 (pbk.)
    1. Marriage. 2. Conflict management. 3. Personality.
4. Negotiation. I. Title.
HQ734.A536 1995
646.7'8—dc20   94–49081
                                     CIP

Printed in the United States of America
1 2 3 4 5 6 7 — 01 00 99 98 97 96 95

Dedication

To my grandparents, Thomas and Catherine;
to my parents, Tom and Dorothy;
to my sister and brother-in-law, Catherine and Glenn;
and of course to my wife, Donna,
with all my love.

Note: The four couples above have been
married a total of 122 years.

Contents

Preface

After my first two books, *Personality Selling* and *Personality Negotiating: Conflict Without Casualty,* came out, I decided to embark on this book. With all of the books that advocate New Age techniques to help relationships blossom, I'm glad you chose *The Fight-Free Marriage.*

Before I get to the heart of this work, I want you to know several important things. First, every example in the book is real, with real people. As a therapist, I know that confidentiality is of the utmost importance. So that you can benefit from the experience of others, while protecting the rights of my clients, I have disguised the cases; I have been careful to retain their meaning, however.

The second disclosure I must make is something that I discovered while writing chapter 11. And that is that Christians don't agree on much theologically. In fact, there is just a handful of ideas that we do agree on. Jesus as God and Savior, the existence of the Trinity, and Jesus' resurrection are it. Beyond that, there are not many ideas that all Christians will embrace as their own. We do agree on ministry in some form and Eucharist in some form. The form and its importance vary widely from denomination to denomination and from Christian to Christian.

I have kept that in mind, and I have included the spectrum of views of various denominations for you to get a feel of how your beliefs match up with those of various other Christians.

Third, many couples feel that fighting or arguing is necessary in a relationship, which it isn't. A good fight is a contradiction in terms—the same as having a good case of the flu. Many feel the alternative, not fighting or arguing, to be too good to be true. By the time they finish the book, they realize that a fight-free marriage is not only possible; it is wonderful.

Fourth, if my book helps you, let me know. A joy of being an author is that I know that my writing helps many people. The problem is, I don't know who you are. If you have a few minutes, drop a line to me in care of Thomas Nelson. I promise to respond to each letter.

Finally, may the words of my lips and the inspiration of my heart be ever acceptable in Your sight, my Lord and my Redeemer.

Tom Anastasi

How Conflict Without Casualty Works

CHAPTER ONE

How is married life treating you?" a honeymooning couple I know were recently asked. "It's great," they answered confidently. "All your friends come to visit you, everyone you know gives you a present, you have a big party, and then you take a vacation."

The reply came with a smirk, "Just wait. You don't know the half of it. *It's a lot of work.* You come home from one job and you've got another one waiting for you . . . and you don't get paid for the second one."

Being committed to your mate doesn't have to be indentured servitude. And that's why Conflict Without Casualty™ was developed.

Conflict Without Casualty™, the combination of psychology and relationship negotiation skills, shows married couples how to appreciate, understand, and relate to each other with love, passion, and vitality. It also shows engaged couples how to prepare the foundation for a life of appreciation and understanding.

Conflict Without Casualty has four parts: (1) you, (2) your mate, (3) the interaction between the two of you, and (4) a covenant relationship between you two and God. First, you and your mate understand personality characteristics that make you, as individuals, distinctive. Then, you'll learn how these characteristics can form a couple that's stronger than each of the parts. Finally, you'll see how all this works in a relationship designed to be lifelong.

There are five billion or so of us in the world, and each of us is different. Yet we share some characteristics with others. That is true of you and your spouse or fiancé. Conflict Without Casualty shows you how to make the most of the similarities. It also shows how each can complement the other with diversity.

THE FIRST GOAL IS
UNDERSTANDING EACH OTHER

The first way Conflict Without Casualty benefits a relationship is by helping the two people understand and appreciate each other. You do this by using your natural observation skills and communication ability to notice new things about yourself and about your mate. During couples' seminars, even partners who have known each other for years are aghast at what they discover:

> I've been living with my wife Joan for fifteen years and never knew she wanted to be by herself for a few minutes when she got home from work.

A wonderful part of teaching Conflict Without Casualty seminars is having people tell me that they were up all night talking about all the things they never knew about each other. It serves as a reminder and reinforcer of the qualities that made two strangers friends and lovers for life.

Have you wondered why some people are much easier to be around than others? People with personalities similar to yours see things as you do, so your styles merge and communication flows easily. You treat them as they want to be dealt with and vice versa. Those who don't share your personality traits see things differently, and you have to work much harder to get your message through and to appreciate what they're saying.

Both mates seldom have the same personality type. With Conflict Without Casualty, you can discover these different traits and modify your approach accordingly. Your negotiation style will click with that of your spouse.

THE SECOND GOAL IS SETTING A STRUCTURE
FOR COLLABORATIVE CONFLICT RESOLUTION

Conflict Without Casualty also involves providing a structure for collaborative problem solving and negotiation.

Many people view conflict as the dark side of a relationship. It's no wonder. To them, conflict means having a battle of wills, feeling nausea at the prospect of disharmony, being weakened, or feeling overly responsible.

Relationship negotiation eliminates the hurtfulness of conflict and replaces it with collaborative problem solving. Solving problems collaboratively produces results that are optimal for you and your mate. Because everyone wins, your relationship is not only preserved but also enhanced. A lack of relationship negotiation can lead to animosity, the breakdown of communication, and the weakening or destruction of a loving relationship.

Conflict Without Casualty shows you how your and your mate's conflict resolution styles and personalities interact. People resolve conflicts—any conflicts—in a predictable pattern. We first learned our conflict resolution patterns when we were about two— from one of our parents. For instance, a two-year-old sees his parents arguing. Time after time, after a heated conversation, one stalks off and says, "I don't care what you do." That toddler thinks to himself, *This is how to solve problems.* When that two-year-old argues with his little friends, he gets into a brief yelling match and then stalks off saying, "I don't care what you do."

You take those early learned patterns into adulthood with you. And though you are much more intelligent and mature, the patterns are the same until you change them to constructive patterns. This book will show you how.

Understanding how these personality traits influence behavior lets you adapt your negotiating style to your partner's. The result is that you'll both find dealing with each other easier and more fruitful. Conflict will be a call to cooperate and improve each other's life instead of a call to arms. The agreements forged will be the best they can be for both parties.

Conflict Resolution Is Not a Battle of Wills
Conflict resolution is the antithesis of a battle of wills. In a battle, the idea is to get as much as you can and give up as little as possible. That's a prescription for unhappiness or imbalance in a marriage.

One of the most destructive myths is that conflict resolution through negotiation is the art of compromise. When you use the collaborative problem-solving principles of Conflict Without Casualty, you'll seldom need to compromise. The vast majority of the time, you can invent a solution together that fully benefits all.

You and your mate accomplish this by discovering what's behind each other's concerns, wants, fears, and desires. The ingredients of a successful negotiation are knowing what each other wants and developing strategies for change that will benefit both of you. Instead of engaging in a tug-of-war with two people pulling at opposite ends of a verbal rope, you and your mate work together.

Negotiation Skills Are Usually a Last Resort

When two people first meet, not too much conflict needs to be negotiated. The beginning stages of a relationship are marked with wild attraction: each person's goal is to please and discover as much as possible about the other. And that spirit of benevolence is contagious. Hormones sloshing around do a great job of allowing you to ignore negative evidence about your new love. What M. Scott Peck calls "the feeling of love," or that tremendous emotional high you get from being unconditionally accepting and accepted of and by another is in full gear. (Real love, according to Peck, begins when infatuation wears off. Real love is a decision to commit oneself to another; it is not a feeling of any kind.)[1]

When you get married, responsibilities change. As a single person, you had control over your time, finances, and living conditions, and you could pretty much do as you pleased. If your spouse, who was your boyfriend or girlfriend at that time, didn't like something, there was not much he or she could say.

> Bart leaves his supper dishes in the sink overnight to wash in the morning. He feels he is too tired from work to do them after dinner. When he and Lucy first started dating, she thought it was a "cute," albeit disgusting, habit. Anyway, it was his apartment. What could she say?

When two people get engaged, they sometimes get their first taste of what negotiating conflicts is all about because resources start becoming scarce and choices need to be made. For instance, your dream wedding will cost twenty-five thousand dollars, and you have ten thousand dollars to spend. What gets cut, and who decides? Or one of you wants to live in the city, the other the suburbs. One wants to buy a condo; the other would rather rent an apartment and save for a house. Books like *Dear Abby on Planning Your Wedding*[2] are filled with horror stories about family members on both sides making life very difficult for the newlyweds-to-be. Most couples tend to spend their betrothal fighting or compromising about wedding plans, and they never learn how to negotiate with each other.

> Bart and Lucy are due to be married in a few weeks. They've decided to live in Lucy's condo. She is worried about the dinnertime dishes in her kitchen crusting overnight. Bart tells her not to worry—they'll be spending most of their time after dinner in bed anyway.

After two people get married, they figure until death do they part is a long way off so they better start expressing their likes and dislikes. There is no more sweeping problems under the rug. They need to use collaborative problem solving. But instead, some go back to the same old same old that they used with their siblings, parents, or people at work: force, invoke guilt, give in, cry, get upset, compromise, criticize, threaten, sabotage, or yell. For every action there's an equal and opposite reaction. For example, one partner using guilt kicks in the threaten response from the other.

> *Guilt Invoker:* If you don't want to see my family, that's all right. (Sob) We see your family a lot. That's all.
> *Threaten Response:* Let's see your family. And when we get there, I'll tell them what a jerk you are.

Here's another variation: yelling brings out crying in a partner. And in return, crying causes giving in. Instead of collaborative problem solving, it looks something like this:

Partner A is bothered and yells at Partner B. Partner B begins to cry. Partner A doesn't like Partner B crying and says, "Fine! Have it your way."

The emotion and energy are being directed at each other rather than being channeled toward a common solution. Also, as we'll see in more detail later, this couple has set up a conflict pattern. Anytime there's something to discuss, A yells, B cries, and A gives in. A is not happy about giving in and avoids conflict altogether or looks to get even with sabotage.

Using relationship negotiation skills, the partners know when they're using hurtful techniques, and they replace them with a collaborative problem-solving approach that works.

When Partner A is bothered, he finds the right time and discovers the proper way of discussing an issue. Then Partner B explains her concerns in an impersonal way, and they invent solutions together.

What's the Catch?

You'll find, with some practice, mutually beneficial agreements will flow smoothly and easily in the vast majority of situations. Coming to this type of agreement is easy assuming that you and your mate: (1) verbalize your desires, (2) listen to what's being said and notice what's not being said, (3) understand and appreciate each other, and (4) desire collaborative solutions.

The catch, if there is one, is that both people are not always motivated negotiators; that is, they don't want a mutually beneficial agreement. The two most common reasons are these: (1) they're still dealing with leftovers (upset about nonrelated subjects that need to be dealt with), or (2) they would rather avoid any kind of conflict than negotiate.

In the chapters ahead, we'll cover in detail how to deal with the motivated and the nonmotivated negotiators. People often get discouraged because they feel they're at an impasse. If that's the case with you, you'll learn many ways to break the standoff.

Here's an example of how Lucy and Bart handled their conflict in an ineffective way:

Lucy and Bart have been married about a month now. Bart is crazy about Lucy and wants to make love with her right after dinner every night. He has made a couple of attempts to wash dishes, but he is too tired after his long commute for mundane activities like housework.

At first, Lucy liked being swept off her feet and pampered in bed. After a couple of weeks, infatuation started wearing off, and her attention turned to plates and silverware with food on them.

To "preserve" harmony, Lucy ends up doing the dishes, but she is starting to feel like she is Bart's maid. Besides, she prepared dinner. Can't he spend a few minutes cleaning up? And there are coffee cups and snack dishes all around too. She wants to make love with Bart, but she feels anxious about the dishes and tells Bart she is "not in the mood."

Bart's conflict resolution style is (1) stew for a while, then (2) attack or criticize, and (3) get even later. Lucy's style is (1) compromise, and (2) avoid. When she is personally assaulted, she reacts by feeling hurt and withdrawing. She figures (incorrectly) she is so hurt that if she discusses the subject, it will only worsen the situation. Let's look at the outcome of *not* using Conflict Without Casualty techniques:

Bart thinks that Lucy is withholding sex to manipulate him into doing dishes. He is very upset that after a long commute, he has to spend time in the kitchen. He always cleans up in the morning, and who cares if there are a few dishes in the sink? You can't see them from the bedroom anyway.

The more he thinks about it, the angrier he gets. All he can think about is that Lucy is becoming just like Debby, his ex-girlfriend, who was always manipulating him too.

Lucy is accustomed to having a neat and clean house. She spends a lot of time cleaning, and she even keeps up with chores she hates doing, like the bathroom. When things are out of place, especially dirty dishes in the sink, she feels uncomfortable. To her it's like having someone scratch fingernails on a blackboard.

She figures that if she always cleans up, Bart will get used to it, and she wants shared responsibility of housework.

After hearing that Lucy isn't in the mood, Bart shouts out: "I can't believe you're using sex as a weapon. You're being just like Debby."

Lucy is hurt by this and doesn't like being compared to Debby. She absolutely doesn't like being accused of using sex as a weapon. She thinks, *If he would just spend a few minutes helping out, I would be happy.* Instead of discussing the situation with Bart, she withdraws.

In the next few days, she does the dishes, but she is angry with Bart. And she is not interested in making love. Bart sees this as a further attempt at control and uses wet-blanket power to sabotage things Lucy likes doing, like visiting friends. The meaner Bart gets, the more Lucy withdraws.

The honeymoon is definitely over. Both Lucy and Bart are casualties of the battle of wills. The cycle continues until they begin using relationship negotiation and appreciation skills.

Here is how a more effective result was achieved by using Conflict Without Casualty techniques:

The first part of the solution involves Bart and Lucy understanding how their personality types interact when they get home. Bart finds out that being organized is very important to Lucy. To him if dirty dishes are out of sight, they're out of mind, but to her the dishes are on her mind, in sight or not.

Lucy discovers that Bart isn't trying to manipulate her into doing housework. She learns that Bart's job as computer manager forces him to be involved in highly detailed work and impromptu meetings with programmers all day. When he gets home, he is beat and needs to charge his battery.

Bart learns that although she is reluctant to mention it, Lucy doesn't like comparisons to his old girlfriends. Also, certain events need to take place before she is relaxed. One of those events happens to be a clean kitchen.

It hits Lucy for the first time that her condo is now *their* condo. It's as much Bart's sink as it is hers. She also learns that

Bart doesn't have a hidden agenda and is not at all interested in her doing an inequitable share of housework. He's just being himself.

Now that Bart and Lucy have an understanding of the situation, they can begin to invent options that take care of their needs.

First, Bart and Lucy need to understand their conflict patterns and replace their destructive methods with effective ones. Instead of stewing and attacking, Bart tells Lucy, "I have a concern, and that concern is . . ."

Every time Lucy is upset and wants to withdraw, she tells Bart, "I have a concern that I want to discuss with you."

Next, they start inventing solutions to their current problem: dishes. Now that they're working together instead of being adversaries, they come up with several good solutions: (1) Bart's doing the dishes after he has had time to relax, but not right after dinner, (2) going out to dinner during the week, (3) eating nonmessy foods like sandwiches, (4) buying disposable cups and plates, and (5) buying a dishwasher with some of their wedding money.

Finally, they discuss other chores and find that Bart doesn't mind doing bathrooms, which he can do during the weekend. Their negotiated solution is trading chores completely. Lucy gets the dishes and Bart gets the bathrooms. Both are happy.

Mutually Beneficial Solutions Don't Always Jump Out at You

Collaborative solutions like Bart and Lucy's are not always this straightforward, but they often are. Reaching mutually beneficial options is possible because each has needs and can give of self in ways the other person cannot. Sometimes the issue is money. It can also be time, attention, effort, accommodation, understanding, or appreciation. Sometimes the answer is right there in front of you, and sometimes it's not. Every negotiation isn't torment, but for the ones that are, Conflict Without Casualty focuses your efforts to win-win solutions.

Throughout the book, you'll learn step-by-step techniques for adapting how you interact with your mate in practical real-life situations.

CONFLICT WITHOUT CASUALTY'S
FOUR PERSONALITY AREAS

There are four areas in which personality theory in Conflict Without Casualty can help.

1. *How Communication Flows Most*
   Comfortably and Effectively

   Janice asks her husband, George, if he has any concerns about her plans to buy a new car. After a good amount of time, he hasn't said anything. She tells him, "Great," and buys an expensive car because he doesn't have any concerns. Did he have any? (The answer is in chapter 3.)

2. *How Many Details People Like Before They Decide*
   and How Much Organization They Want

   Fred and Laurie are talking about what house they want to buy. Fred wants to peruse the multiple-listing books and look only at the house they finally decide on. Will Laurie feel the same way? (The answer is in chapter 4.)

3. *How People Develop Concerns, Express Emotions,*
   and How They View Relationships

   Tracy mentioned to Paul before they were married that she hoped she would always be the same weight. Every time she loses or gains a few pounds he mentions it. Is Tracy appreciative of Paul's concern? (The answer is in chapter 5.)

14. *What Perspective People Have About*
    Time When They Make a Decision

   Boris wants to decide where to go on vacation before the end of the month. Cathy, his wife, is still looking at guidebooks. What should they do? (The answer is in chapter 6.)

   In the coming chapters, you'll find that the answers to these and other everyday situations differ depending on the temperament of your mate.

THE PERSONALITY THEORY IS PROVEN IN PSYCHOLOGY

A key to predicting others' behavior is using personality theory. The personality theory we'll use is based on Carl Jung's work on personality type.[3] Jungian personality type is measured in many ways, the two most common being the Keirsey and Bates temperament sorter and the Myers-Briggs Type Indicator (MBTI)®.[4] The Jungian personality type is used in family therapy, premarital counseling, management development, and sales. Two psychologists, Isabel Myers and Katherine Briggs, developed the MBTI to help people appreciate each other better. The MBTI has been used for over forty years and has been validated in hundreds of scientific studies. The MBTI and other Jungian personality type measures have been used over two million times.[5]

Many haven't heard of Jungian personality traits or the MBTI, and they're unaware of the value to couples. Conflict Without Casualty, using the MBTI, describes and categorizes behavior four ways, with each category, or index, having two alternative preferences for a total of eight separate preferences. These eight preferences (and their single letter abbreviations) are:

Introvert (I) or Extrovert (E)	Sensing (S) or Intuitive (N)	Thinking (T) or Feeling (F)	Judging (J) or Perceiving (P)
How we interact with others— our communication preferences.	How we process information and what motivates conflict.	How we develop concerns and relate to people.	Our view of time and how we make decisions.

THE EIGHT PREFERENCES

Here is a brief overview of the eight preferences and their individual relevance in negotiations. The preferences will be covered in detail and in combinations in the upcoming chapters with examples of their usefulness in your relationship.

First is the Introvert/Extrovert index (see chapter 3). It's useful when choosing how and when to communicate with others.

Introverts like to analyze information alone and consider questions before they speak. Make sure you allow a balance of couple time and private time. Also, when you ask Introverts questions, wait for answers.

Extroverts like to be in a group, and they enjoy discussing ideas. Make sure they have a lot of social time, and discuss ideas with them instead of having them ponder alone.

Second is the Sensing/Intuitive index (see chapter 4). It is especially useful when you decide on the content of supporting data in discussions and on the person to take care of tasks involving details and organization.

Sensing types are convinced by data rich in facts, and they want answers to problems to have practical benefits; they'll notice every detail. They crave organization and like it when people and their environment are pleasing to their senses. Give them what they want: facts, details, practicality, structure, and an attractive environment.

Intuitives need to know the theory behind an idea, and they don't want much detail. Speak with them in terms of the big picture, and don't get bogged down in details.

Third is the Thinking/Feeling index (see chapter 5). It comes into play when you're ironing out differences, expressing emotions, and understanding interpersonal relationships.

Thinking types make decisions objectively and analytically. They tend to make suggestions impersonally. Stress the logical reasons for their accepting what's important to you.

Feeling types make decisions based on improving the quality of people's lives. They tend to take suggestions personally. You can maintain harmony by not being critical or insensitive to the needs of others.

Fourth is the Judging/Perceiving index (see chapter 6). The Judging/Perceiving index is the key indicator to how people decide and how they view time.

Judging types like making schedules and deadlines and keeping to them. When you plan with Judging types, respect and try to keep to their schedules. If their schedules are getting in the way, help them make new schedules.

Perceiving types like flexible schedules and deadlines, and they are careful decision makers. Be flexible with the Perceiving types. They will be event driven, not time driven. Discovering and addressing key events that need to happen before they're comfortable will move things along.

According to Jungian theory, each of us leans toward one of the two preferences in each of the four indexes. The four index preferences, collectively, indicate personality type. (There are sixteen variations of personality types. For example, one is an Extroverted, Sensing, Thinking, Judging type [ESTJ].)

MOST PEOPLE ARE UNAWARE OF THEIR PREFERENCES

Many of us are unaware we have the preferences listed above, though we all do. For instance, Judging types will plan a big family purchase, like a pool, for years and get one when the time has come. Perceiving types will decide that they're hot and that they have some extra money in the bank; they will buy a pool in a few days. Although both ways are different, neither way is better. Judging types could spend several sticky summers before it's "time" to buy a pool, and Perceiving types might buy one that's too small. Making people act outside their type is like making left-handers write with the right hand. They can do it, but it won't be natural, easy, or fun.

The tendency is to negotiate the way we want others to negotiate with us. The problem is that this works only with people just like us.

Strategies that work well with one type of person in your life, your boss, for example, may or may not work with others. That's why you can't do cookie-cutter negotiations (negotiate the same way every time). With Conflict Without Casualty, you'll know how to, when to, and in what ways to deal with your partner in all types of situations. Each day will be as stress free as possible.

Negotiation for Married and Engaged Couples

CHAPTER TWO

Conflict Without Casualty Helps You Go the Distance

When two people play the mating game, especially at the start of a relationship, they feel appreciated, wanted, vital, and desirable. When the relationship proceeds to newlywed status, the partners experience a new level of joy as the thrill of willingly accepting and being accepted blocks any thought of discontent. Hormones sloshing around shout that the partner is the most attractive person on earth. While infatuated, both partners use terms like *God's gift* and *perfect* to describe their love.

They look with bewilderment at some seasoned couples whose ongoing, unresolved conflicts are like a cancer destroying the relationship, and they think, *This will never happen to us!* It doesn't have to. The key is to practice collaborative problem solving so animosities don't build up. Collaborative problem solving not only avoids damaging a new relationship but also reverses strain and resentment in an established relationship. Couples who are hurting because of poor conflict resolution skills can learn to successfully problem solve and fix much damage that's been done and heal the relationship.

In this chapter, I'll set up a model for conflict resolution that I'll be expanding throughout the book. Here, I'll look at negotiation and conflict resolution skills that are useful for your relationship with your mate and other important relationships in your life.

Many consider conflict a necessary evil in any relationship. And it's no wonder. Until people know how to handle conflict, it can bring out the worst—they can become withdrawn or belligerent. It doesn't have to be that way. When we get frustrated or feel backed into a corner, we can do collaborative problem solving. Collaboration is a skill that we can learn. Most people don't collaborate; they invoke the fight-or-flight response. Just as it sounds, that's the part of the brain that says to avoid the conflict or attack the other party.

A significant element in collaborative problem solving is knowing when your brain kicks in the attack-or-avoid process and opting for a more effective method. It's easy to learn and takes practice, but once you become good at it, it comes naturally.

CONFLICT RESOLUTION STYLE IS PREDICTABLE

As I stated earlier, each of us learned a conflict resolution style at a very early age. We watched our parents, one in particular, and observed what they said or did—how they reacted—when there was a conflict. Even though as adults we are more mature, many of us have not changed the conflict resolution patterns that we established as youngsters.

Many of the people that I train in conflict resolution—from lawyers at the University of Washington to employees of Fortune 500 corporations—usually have the ineffective conflict resolution patterns that they learned in the family of origin. The average age of these people is thirty-five to fifty, and for the most part, my seminar is their first exposure to conflict resolution.

As a therapist, I deal with all ages. During premarital counseling, I am fortunate to teach people about conflict resolution at the early stages of a relationship because then they can avoid many serious problems.

The good news is that since conflict resolution style is learned, people can learn other patterns that are effective with all types of people in all situations.

Roger Fisher and William Ury of Harvard University's Negotiation Project wrote a great book called *Getting to Yes: Negotiating Agreement Without Giving In*. Fisher and Ury were the pioneers in making conflict resolution a serious science. They separated conflict behavior into three categories: hard, soft, and collaborative. Since then, Robert Benfari and others have expanded hard into two styles (win-lose and compromise) and soft into two styles (yield-lose and lose-lose), so that together with collaborative there are a total of five styles.[1]

LET'S LOOK AT THE STYLES

Each of us has a consistent order in which we use styles of conflict, as I'll describe below. Match up the descriptions to how you solve conflicts to get your style.

Hard Style

People with a hard style not only make life difficult for others but also have a difficult life. When faced with a conflict, they feel the need to take control, have the answers, and be right. They see to it that their solution is the only one discussed or implemented. They feel that if this is not the case, others will not respect them or value their skill or competence.

Often they say that they listen to others, but they don't. Sometimes they make no bones about the fact they don't want to listen. The rallying cries of people with a hard style sound like this: "There are two ways of doing things, my way and the wrong way," and "It's my way or the highway."

People have a hard style not because they want to alienate others, though that is frequently the outcome. They're worried that if they give up control and allow others to resolve the conflict, disaster will strike. And they may also have self-image difficulties since they associate being right with competence, intelligence, and so forth.

To avoid what they perceive as negative aspects of interpersonal relationships, they seek as much control in their domain as they can. Of course, having total control is impossible, but they try.

After a while, two events are likely. The first involves the well-being of the people with a hard style. Since control has both psychological and physiological impacts, the pressure they put on themselves will start to take a toll in the forms of stress, anxiety, loss of sleep, and a lesser quality of life. The second involves relationships with other people. An unwanted side effect of having a hard style is that those who are controlled tend to feel resentful. (Later on, I'll split hard styles into two types, win-lose and compromise.)

Soft Style

People with a soft style dread conflict and avoid it at all cost. Their fear is that conflict brings animosity, and then important relationships will suffer or end. The irony in this thinking is that eventually such avoiders will get tired of being a doormat and will usually see no way out other than to break up with the person they've been avoiding. The very relationships they're trying to sustain by avoidance are doomed—until they stop avoiding.

Avoidance can take as many forms as there are avoiders. Avoiders can remove themselves from a room, shun certain topics, make light of subjects that concern them greatly, be involved in activities not associated with the mate, or nod yes when they mean no, among countless other ways to temporarily stay out of conflict.

Avoiders can also give the outward appearance of not avoiding while avoiding internally.

Fay and Jeff have been married for three months. They met six months before they got married, and Jeff still gets calls from old girlfriends. One called and left a message wanting to know if he would like to go to Vermont with her for the weekend.

Fay informed her that "his wife" would probably not approve of that, and the woman felt embarrassed and told Fay that she didn't know that Jeff had been married.

Fay doesn't want Jeff to think that she is jealous, so she doesn't say anything. However, she gets anxious every time the phone rings or she doesn't pick up the mail because perfumed letters keep arriving. Since Jeff hasn't mentioned anything, Fay is worried that he is hedging his bet and continuing to keep contact with these women just in case the marriage doesn't work out.

Her parents warned her against the whirlwind wedding, and now she is having doubts. Still, she doesn't want to broach the subject for fear that Jeff will confirm her fears.

Anytime Jeff receives a phone call or letter, he always returns it, letting the woman know that he fell in love and got married. He dated quite a bit before he met Fay, and he doesn't let Fay know that he is being contacted for fear that she would feel that she had competition. His father warned him that impulsive marriages can leave spouses feeling uneasy that former flames have not died out.

Both Jeff and Fay are avoiding the conflict.

Collaborative Style
Hard and soft are not the only choices in handling conflict. There is another, collaborative. In collaborative problem solving you think of and list all of the things that are important to you, called concerns. Your mate does the same. Once you have discovered all of the vital concerns, you think of ways that they can be met for both of you. Then together you choose the best options and think of ways to implement solutions that are best for everyone.

This can be quite challenging at first. It's a temptation to proceed as usual and either give in or avoid when a satisfying solution becomes evasive or seemingly out of reach.

Collaborative problem solving involves talking, listening, thinking, and working together. Threats, intimidation, and physical force are definite no-no's. So are leaving, ignoring, and not listening.

When Jeff and Fay finally started problem solving, they realized that a collaborative solution was easy. Fay put a message on the answering machine saying, "This is Fay and Jeff Keitzer. Leave a message and we'll get back to you." That way callers would know that Jeff was married.

Also, Jeff said that he would tell Fay when he got a call or letter from an old girlfriend, and he would assure her that he was cutting his ties with her. Relieved by this solution, Fay was not as bothered by the number of calls and letters coming because it was Christmas season. She now knew that natural attrition would occur in time.

That's it! The key is to learn methods for implementing collaborative problem solving. Many people know intuitively what needs to be done, either with their mate or with other family members. For instance, someone may know that he wants to discuss parental control with the in-law parents. He knows intellectually that he should call his mother-in-law and list everyone's concerns and develop solutions that are best for everyone. Still, he would rather die than have that conversation, so the misery goes on.

I'll show you how to deal with all types of conflicts in all situations. Armed with a knowledge of personality type, conflict styles, and patterns, you'll know how and when to approach people, what information to use, how they develop concerns, and how they make decisions. And you'll find that resolutions are not difficult and your fears usually are far outweighed by the benefits.

Some people think that collaborative problem solving is a boring alternative to verbal sparring. Once they realize that the price of admission to verbal fighting is the loss or deterioration of important relationships, the thrill of the fight goes away.

WE CAN SWITCH AMONG STYLES

An aspect of conflict resolution is that no one has a pure style 100 percent of the time. We can shift from hard to soft to collaborative back to soft, and we tend to do so in a predictable order or pattern. We need to understand the changes and observe how people react.

For example, someone may have a soft conflict resolution style and avoid most conflicts. However, when that person is confronted with an issue of importance to her, she will switch the style to either a hard style or a collaborative style, depending on the personal pattern. If that style doesn't work, she will change it again until the conflict is resolved.

Conflicts are usually resolved by the third shift in style, but we can shift as many as five times, though that's rare. People who have a hard-soft-hard-soft-collaborative style, for instance, will never get to collaborative in most negotiations because they've avoided or attacked so long that the conflict is (at least on the surface) long over. We can switch from hard to soft more than once, but we generally are in the collaborative stage only once. Then if that doesn't work, we give up and try a different, less effective style. Knowing about this pattern is integral to changing it. If you find yourself in a stage that isn't effective, or if you realize that you are leaving the collaborative stage, force yourself to get back in the collaborative groove.

Here are some examples:

Soft-hard-soft. This person avoids conflict, but if he feels that people are taking advantage of him, or if the subject is important to him, he'll think, *Forget it. We're doing it my way.* If that doesn't work, he'll get fed up with the whole process and give up.

Soft-hard-collaborative. This style is similar to soft-hard-soft. The difference is that after trying to force her way, rather than giving up and giving in, she will focus on solutions that are good for everyone.

Soft-collaborative-hard. This person will avoid conflicts but then try to get solutions that are good for everyone. If that doesn't work, he'll think to himself, *I didn't even want to deal with this, and then I tried to work out a solution that's good for everyone. That didn't work. Now we're going to do it my way.*

Hard-soft-hard. This person wants conflict to be solved her way. If that doesn't work, she'll think, *Forget it. Do it your way.* That's normally where the conflict will end because the people she deals with will jump at the opportunity to "win" one. However, if the other person's solution is viewed as too one-sided, a hard-soft-hard person goes back to the hard style. The thinking is that she allowed the other side to come up with a fair deal, but he wasn't interested, so now it's her way.

Hard-soft-collaborative. The hard-soft-collaborative attributes are the same as the hard-soft-hard with the difference that after going through the attacking and avoiding, the person searches for answers that benefit everyone if the conflict hasn't been resolved.

Collaborative. If you start off collaborative, that's great. Still, a trait of people who start off collaborative is that if others aren't immediately collaborative, too, they switch to their next style quickly. When this happens, force yourself to keep at it so everyone wins.

Collaborative-hard-soft. This person starts by developing collaborative solutions to problems. If the solutions are not present, or if he is dealing with people who do not want collaborative solutions, the tendency is to give up and take over. If that doesn't work, she thinks, *I can't stand this anymore,* and walks away.

Collaborative-soft-hard. This person will try collaborative problem solving. If that's not successful, this person will get frustrated and say, "Do it your way." If that doesn't work, or the solution is unfair, he'll say, "Forget it. We're doing it my way."

WHAT TO DO IF YOUR PARTNER
IS IN A DIFFERENT STYLE

People with hard styles tend to find people with soft styles. When this situation exists, one person takes control, and the other has decisions made for him or her. Or both avoid conflict and go weeks or months or years without talking about conflict or talking at all.

When you use the techniques in Conflict Without Casualty for collaborative problem solving, but your partner is either in the hard style (wants a deal with only personal benefits) or in the soft style (wants to avoid the entire situation), you keep focusing on your concerns and those of your partner until he or she is in the collaborative mode.

If the first three styles employed are hard-soft-hard, you and your mate will have to go through all three stages before anything collaborative can happen. The fourth style may be soft, and you have to keep struggling. When your mate is finally in the collaborative mode, you can use that opportunity to get a win-win outcome.

You'll find that with practice, your spouse's style will change, and collaboration will occur more readily.

A Hard-Soft Combination

A fascinating aspect of human behavior is how we choose a spouse. When we are single, we see hundreds of members of the opposite sex every day who appeal to us. Yet we somehow narrow our choices to one lucky person and decide to stay with that person for life.

Psychologists frequently try to make sense of male-female relations by evaluating statistics of large groups of similar people and determining whether trends form. The technical term for this is *macroanalysis*.

Macroanalysis has taught us that one partner with a hard style and one with a soft style are common. One person wants to take charge, and the other wants someone else to take control. Often, one partner has turmoil in life and finds comfort in someone else making the decisions.

The person with a hard conflict resolution style seeks someone who wants another person to guide and take control of major decisions.

The intent is not to set up a dependent-authoritarian relationship, but that's often what happens. Also, years later in the relationship, the person with the hard style gets tired of being overly responsible. More often, the person with the soft style gets frustrated at the mate making all the decisions and says, "I feel suffocated," or "I want to grow." The person is saying, "I no longer need you to make decisions for me, and I want to do it on my own."

The problem is that after so many years of having others make decisions for her, the avoider doesn't know how to decide or, at first, isn't very good at it. Still, she has a burning desire to be responsible for her own destiny.

Kelly is a forty-two-year-old mother of two. In therapy she lamented, "I was in high school, and my parents made all my decisions. Right after high school I got married and moved in with Peter. Peter was responsible for the checkbook and made all the decisions. He's a wonderful man, but I realized that I have been doing what everyone else wanted all my life. I want to make decisions. I want to be wrong every now and then. I want to find out who I am and what I'm capable of doing."

Kelly's concerns are felt by many people. Kelly has an overwhelming wish to find her true capabilities. She was a conflict avoider but doesn't want to be anymore.

The best place for Kelly to "find herself" and "grow" is in the relationship with Peter. Many psychologists would encourage Kelly to get divorced. They would "empower" her to leave her husband and be independent. Unfortunately, many psychologists do not respect enduring values and the sanctity of marriage. They view dating, engagement, and marriage as the same, which they are not.

An Avoider-Avoider Combination

The second most common form of relationship is one where both members of the couple are conflict avoiders. Neither likes conflict, and both are happy to have the appearance of harmony. Linda and Gerald avoid conflict:

Gerald and I are excellent at solving conflict. We have known each other for seven years. We have never had an argument, and we have never raised our voices to each other.

Linda and Gerald found out six months later that such an approach is a recipe for disaster. One day all of their pent-up hostilities came out, and they were overwhelmed. They broke up, and each found a new conflict avoider.

A Hard-Hard Combination

Couples where both have a hard, adversarial style are rare because they don't date very long. Since both are vying for control and one-upmanship in the relationship, they often get frustrated dealing with each other and break up.

When hard-hard couples stay together, as you can imagine, a lot of arguing goes on. Each partner is always trying to be in control and trying to be right. These couples generally want to learn collaboration because both agree that all the arguing is unsatisfying. In couples with only one having a hard style, sometimes that takes longer.

A Collaboration-Collaboration Combination

Since only one person in one hundred is a collaborative problem solver, only about one in ten thousand couples are collaborative-collaborative. (Although after training and reading books like this, couples can learn win-win conflict resolution and become collaborative-collaborative.)

TWO TYPES OF HARD STYLES

After a while, you'll be able to notice two types of hard styles. The first one is win-lose. Someone wants a deal that is good only for her and not for the other person. When win-lose happens in the first stages of the conflict, one person wants to maintain control and is afraid if she surrenders control, terrible events will follow.

When you deal with this type of person, assure him that the world will not come to an end if he gives up control. This will not happen right off the bat because that person will have an entire life's experience of dealing with conflict by taking over. Start small. Let him know that you want to try something, and set a worst-case scenario that he can live with. Little by little he will feel comfortable giving up control, and it will be very freeing for him. It's freeing because maintaining control is very difficult and takes lots of energy. Giving him permission to have others help him out will make his life much easier.

People who have a win-lose style of conflict resolution are fed up with people walking over them and are striking back as best they can. When this is the case, let them know they don't have to strike back, or get them on track by saying you understand they're upset, but you think the situation can be worked out.

The second type of hard style is compromise. Many people new to conflict resolution don't see compromise as a hard style. In fact, many people think that the goal of conflict resolution and negotiation is compromise.

The theory behind compromise is that half the pie is better than none. It's considered a hard style because although you're getting part of what you want, you're giving up part of what you want, and so is your mate.

Once you get proficient at collaborative problem solving you'll find that you don't have to compromise more than once or twice a year in any important relationship.

TWO TYPES OF SOFT STYLES

There are two types of soft styles: yield-lose and lose-lose. In yield-lose, people can't stand the conflict anymore, and they settle for a deal that doesn't benefit them. People with yield-lose style usually give up prematurely. This is unfortunate because they find that if they kept inventing options, they wouldn't have to settle for yield-lose deals.

In lose-lose, both people are unhappy with the outcome—the

theory that misery loves company. Lose-lose occurs when people feel that they can't win, so they don't want other people to win. Again, if people invent options, they find that lose-lose doesn't have to happen.

The consequences of yield-lose and lose-lose, taken to the extreme, can be severe—and they often are. Other options must be chosen. When people are in the yield-lose stage, they can let terrible things happen to them, like giving in sexually so that they feel raped. It can also involve violence. (The appendix, "Conflict Resolution in Abusive Relationships," goes into this subject in more detail.)

CONFLICT RESOLUTION STYLE GETS MAGNIFIED

The initial conflict resolution style gets magnified during dating. Remember, people with a soft conflict resolution style have it because they are mistakenly afraid that if they challenge someone, the relationship will suffer or end.

> Ron and Francie had been dating for three years before they got married. Neither of them smoked, but three of Francie's friends smoked. When those friends visited Francie, they would always light up.
>
> Ron hated the cigarette smoke. When he visited Francie at her apartment and her friends came over, he would make an excuse to leave, not telling Francie the reason why, for fear of upsetting her.
>
> Now that they're married, Francie's friends still come over, but now they're smoking at Ron's home.

People with a hard conflict resolution style have misconceptions during the dating stage. They're afraid that if they don't maintain control, situations will get out hand, and the relationship will end.

> While Tom and Ann Marie were dating, Tom always picked out the movies that they saw in theaters. Ann Marie thought movies like *The Terminator* were silly and unrealistic. She preferred going to dramas that received critical acclaim. Tom

thought those movies were boring. He felt that the special effects in the movies that he liked were not as spectacular on video, while her movies never had any special effects so she could rent them for a lot less and get the same enjoyment. However, Ann Marie felt that going to the movies was an event.

In any serious relationship, a couple's major goal is the security of the relationship. That's a valid concern, and using the conflict resolution skills you'll learn in this book will insure it doesn't happen. Conflict Without Casualty works because we peel back the sources of a couple's conflict layer by layer, like an onion. Sometimes there's some crying, but the goal is to get to the heart of the matter. And most of the time the heart is a case of misperception or opposing conflict resolution styles.

A rule of thumb is that arguing is always an available option, but reserve it only as a last resort. Those who use hurtful tactics as trump cards find that they never need to use them, and discovering collaborative solutions is much more fulfilling.

Before getting into specific strategies that you can tailor to your personality and relationship, let's look at the concepts common to all marital negotiations.

MARITAL NEGOTIATION

Marital negotiation is the process by which a married or engaged couple come to a mutually beneficial consensus on both the day-to-day struggles and the major issues that crop up in their lives. The principles can also be good for other close relationships, for example, with family members and friends.

In a marriage each spouse gives what he or she can to get what he or she needs. All successful marital negotiations share one goal: having both parties come out with everything they need to be happy. During the negotiation process, both parties explain their feelings, what they can offer, what they need, and the reasons that the couple will come out ahead after an agreement is reached.

You may not realize it, but you and your partner, whether you're married, engaged, or almost engaged, negotiate many times each day. Not all negotiations are long and complex. For example, when you hold off on using the microwave for a few minutes so your mate can make it to work on time, that's a negotiation.

Many types of negotiations take place in a marriage. The techniques and the process of explaining needs, desires, fears, wants, hopes, dreams, and frustrations are the same for all types of negotiations.

THE NEGOTIATION RECIPE

There are two essential ingredients to a successful marital negotiation. The first needed ingredient is a *feeling that a solution where everybody wins is better than all other outcomes.* The second is arriving at an understanding of the difference between concerns and positions.

INGREDIENT #1: WANTING YOUR SPOUSE TO HAVE EVERYTHING IMPORTANT TO THEM

The first ingredient in collaborative problem solving is the desire of the parties involved to want or need the other person or group in the negotiation to succeed. The following is not a negotiation:

> Greg is an accountant for a large company. His wife, Melissa, takes care of their four children and works at a video rental store a few nights a week. Greg thinks that after all the bills are paid, he should be able to spend the money he makes on extras, and that to avoid problems with bounced checks, they should keep separate checking accounts. Greg takes home about $4,000 per month and pays for most of the vacations for the family as well as all of the major family expenses.
>
> Most of the $35 per week that Melissa takes home goes to buy presents for the children as well as for Greg, though she does occasionally buy herself a CD, new shoes, or some flowers.
>
> Greg doesn't like his job very much, and to make himself feel better about this likes to buy new and fun consumer items. Last month he bought a new sound system, a computerized rowing machine, and a big-screen TV.
>
> Melissa is upset because she wasn't consulted on any of

those purchases and feels that there are more important family expenses to consider. Greg tells her that he's the man and if she didn't go and get pregnant four times, maybe they'd have more money to spend on themselves. If she doesn't like it, then she can leave and try to find someone else who will support her better.

Extreme win/lose situations are never as effective as collaboration, but in a relationship it's particularly ineffective. You don't want to swindle, con, threaten, take advantage of, or hurt someone that you're going to sleep with for the next fifty years.

Unfortunately, when a couple battles like Greg and Melissa, both parties will lose. And, most of the time the winner gets less on the battlefield than he would have at the negotiation table.

Melissa is frustrated with Greg and wants to get him angry. She knows he does not like her wearing sexy clothes, because he's uncomfortable when other men are looking at her.

So, in order to get even, Melissa starts to wear tighter clothes that show off her figure. When that didn't get him mad enough, she stopped wearing the conservative one-piece bathing suit she had been wearing and began using the bikini that she wore while they were dating.

When that didn't work, she bought a thong bikini, which didn't cover any part of her from the back.

When Greg told her that he refused to have her wear that bathing suit, she told him that she would go to the beach with the kids while he was at work. And besides, like he said, each member of the couple could buy what they want with their money.

"If buying sound systems and TVs and rowing machines gives you pleasure, that's okay. Thong bikinis give me pleasure and that's what I'll buy."

Neither Melissa nor Greg is very happy with the situation, but both are stubborn and unwilling to acquiesce. Good negotiation isn't "getting" concessions while "giving up" little. Negotiation isn't debating or battling because rather than having a winner and a loser, good negotiations have two winners.

INGREDIENT #2: UNDERSTANDING AND RESOLVING POSITIONS VERSUS CONCERNS

To make sure that everyone wins, partners need to explain the reasons why their concerns are important to them. Integral to understanding are listening, information gathering, and knowing that a lot behind the concerns needs attention. We're so accustomed to talking about positions, it takes practice to ferret out the concerns of others or even recognize the difference between our own concerns and positions. Let's look at what positions and concerns are and how they're different.

Positions

Positions are opinions and feelings about people, places, things, ideas, or anything else. One must accept another's opinions as the way he feels and not try to change his convictions. You can't negotiate opinions because diverse opinions are equally valid. And you can't convince someone his opinion is wrong because it never is.

If you want to argue about positions, you've got two options—see who can outlast the opponent, or escalate the options by yelling and becoming increasingly hostile. Eventually, someone cracks and you seemingly have a winner and a loser, but in reality you have no winners.

If you and your spouse argue over positions, realize it "ain't" working and try something else. How? Just say that nothing's being accomplished and you need to try something else.

Concerns

Concerns are different from positions. Concerns can be discussed and adapted, unlike opinions, which must be accepted for what they are. Concerns are the reasons behind what we want. One can usually fulfill these desires in many ways.

YOU CAN'T ARGUE OPINION OR FACTS

You can't successfully argue opinions or facts, though couples do for hours, days, or even years. Why? You get into the never-ending sequence of "I think," "No, I think," "You're wrong," "No, you're wrong," and on and on. When you and your partner argue about a fact or an opinion, realize that you've reached an impasse.

If you're arguing about a fact, you have to find a mutually agreeable expert or source to verify the fact.

You need to boil down opinions about issues to their least common denominator, the underlying concern behind them. It takes practice, but after a while you'll be able to recognize the difference. Here are some examples of concerns and opinions:

Opinion	*Concern*
You're spending too much money.	We won't have enough money to pay the electric bill.
I hate it when you drink.	Some behaviors associated with drinking (being argumentative, being hostile, and lack of inhibitions) are bothersome to me. (This should be told to the person when sober.)
I want more sex.	I am very attracted to you and since the only person I can make love with is you, I need your help in sexual release.
You're driving too fast.	You wouldn't have time to stop in case of emergency.

As you can see from the opinion column, each statement can be responded to with a counterposition. "You're spending too much," will be met with "No, I'm not." One person absolutely feels another is overspending, while the other absolutely feels that's not the case. They can argue forever and never come to a resolution. Why? Again, because both are 100 percent right in their positions. Here's an example of this dilemma:

Milt is a twenty-eight-year-old engineer. He bought his Porsche when he was twenty-two, just a few months before meeting Alicia, his wife.

Alicia liked the Porsche, and she realized that Milt spent

a lot of money on it. The car has about a 150,000 miles on it, and the last few years repairs have been expensive.

The last time Milt took his car in for repairs, the garage owners told him that the repairs would be three thousand dollars. Milt and Alicia decided together that was too much to spend on such an old car.

Milt needs a new car. Let's look at how he and Alicia are going to decide which one to buy.

MAKING THE CONNECTION BETWEEN POSITIONS AND CONCERNS

Step 1: Think About What Is Most Important

The first thing Milt needs to do is list all of his concerns; that is, all of the aspects of owning a car that are important to him.

Milt wants a car that

- looks good
- has status
- costs less than four hundred dollars per month in payments
- is a Porsche

Milt suggests to Alicia that he would consider getting a used Porsche in order to keep the payments less than four hundred dollars per month.

Alicia lists her concerns. She wants a car that

- Milt will be happy buying
- is safe for the children to ride in
- the family can afford and perhaps have some extra money by lowering the five-hundred-dollar payments that they're paying now

The garage owners have agreed to pay off what Milt owes on his loan if he sells them his car for parts. [I'll continue this story in a moment.]

Step 2: Educate Each Other, If Necessary, on Concerns

In business negotiations, you need to be careful about the supporting evidence that you bring since you may be called on the carpet at some time to prove your point. In personal negotiations, your goals are different. You want to educate your mate on why your concerns are important and why they are valid, even if you have no charts or statistics to back them up.

Step 3: Invent Options

The next step is to invent options. After understanding each other's concerns, not only from an intellectual standpoint but also from an emotional one, figure out ways that everyone's concerns can be met.

As a therapist or a mediator, I work with couples and help them list their concerns and educate each other. Sometimes couples are set in their routines or have written off any hope of getting what's important to them. Invariably, we are able to give relationships new life, and with a little hard work, they realize that most problems are not insurmountable.

I get a similar response every time I ask people not yet skilled in inventing options, "So, what can we do that will satisfy everyone's concerns?" The responses are: "There's no way," "I guess I'm just going to have to live with this," and "It's impossible" (the most common response).

These couples find that with practice, solutions are possible, and most of the time, they can come up with a collaborative solution. There will be exceptions. Once every couple of years, you'll have to compromise. If you find yourself compromising more often, that's a signal that you have to put more elbow grease into your collaboration.

When you're inventing options, be creative. When you first start inventing options, you may have to make four or five tries, but it's worth it. The payoff is that everyone is happy with the outcome.

The trick is to be open to suggestions and not close out any discussion until you've thought it out. A common trait of inventing options is that the solutions often are quite different from anything you had in mind at first blush. But that's okay because the goal is

to make everyone happy with the result, not to pigeonhole any
particular solution.

Step 4: Assess the Viability of Each Option

Going back to the example of Milt and his Porsche, there are
many possible approaches:

- Alternative 1: Use public transportation. Buses and trains
  don't go far enough or frequently enough for the family.
- Alternative 2: Buy a sports car. Buy a new car just like the
  model he has.
- Alternative 3: Buy a Volvo or minivan. Each is safe, but
  Milt feels that no one will mistake either for a Porsche.
- Alternative 4: Get a horse. Oh, Wilbur!
- Alternative 5: Get a used sports car. It could be economical,
  but safety is still an issue.

By creating these lists, Milt is analyzing the alternatives to
solutions apart from his wanting to have a new Porsche.

Step 5: Decide Together on the Best Alternative

Although Milt originally wanted a new car, he and Alicia need
to analyze their concerns apart from solutions tied to "needs."
Negotiators call this "separating the person from the problem."

Milt and Alicia decided that a used car would be the best
solution economically. Still, Alicia's safety concerns had to be
met.

> After analyzing all the options, Milt and Alicia decided
> that a used Porsche would satisfy all of Milt's concerns and
> all of Alicia's concerns—except for safety.
>
> Milt found a Porsche that was five years old with only
> 35,000 miles on it. The payments would be $350 a month.
> Alicia said that model didn't have air bags, which were a
> concern to her.
>
> Milt thought that the air bags were just a marketing ploy
> and really didn't do anything. Alicia and Milt went to the
> library and did research on air bags. They found that they are

very effective. Still, they weren't mandated in the year the Porsche Milt wanted was built.

After they went to the library, they went to the Porsche dealer and found out whether an air bag could be installed in the model Milt wanted to buy. The dealer said that it could be done, but the cost would put the monthly payments over $400.

When they got home, they got out the phone book and called garages and mechanics and priced installation of an air bag in an older Porsche. The price they got was far less than the dealer and offered the same warranty. The result was that the payments would increase only $20 per month, far below the $400 threshold they both felt comfortable with. So that's what they did.

Separating the Person from the Problem

The authors of *Getting to Yes: Negotiating Agreement Without Giving In,* say to "separate the person from the problem."[2] Couples should focus on the problem instead of their opinions about the problem. Doing that makes the parties focus on concerns and makes resolution easier. Getting emotionally involved in an argument makes it difficult for people to see beyond their strongly held positions.

Once Milt and Alicia started discussing their concerns, they were both on the same side, and the discussion proceeded smoothly. If they had discussed their opinions, they could have argued for hours and gotten nowhere.

We'll apply the general information in this chapter to many examples throughout the book. By the end, you'll know how to apply conflict resolution in any situation.

The next few chapters will discuss personality type. Then we'll look at patterns and conflict resolution for couples who are dating, engaged, and married. You'll find that your relationship will improve and will be lovingly sustained.

Getting Through to Each Other

CHAPTER THREE

Conflict Without Casualty
Opens the Lines

Much of what goes on in premarital counseling is drilling home the message that communication is key to a successful marriage: "When you have differences, let your partner know. And always listen. Good luck in the future." This chapter shows how to do it.

A foundation of Conflict Without Casualty is that healthy relationships are based on good communication patterns. Collaborative solutions begin and end with each party knowing what the other party wants. That sounds easy, but in reality it can be tough. A common complaint in troubled relationships is, "My partner doesn't listen to me anymore." The most chilling aspect of that complaint is that the partner will assert that he or she *is* listening.

Well, something's afoot. The receiving party is not acknowledging listening or is misinterpreting the sender's messages. Since marital communication is a two-way process, no blame can be doled. If you have excellent communication skills, this chapter will give you psychological reinforcement to support why what you're doing is right. If your skills aren't as sharp as they could be, this chapter will help you develop better skills.

The longer two people know each other and the more intimately their lives are intermingled, the *more* they are likely to *assume* what each other means, which hampers communication. As you become more familiar with someone's mannerisms and voice, there is an increased likelihood that your brain will make assumptions. This is true for anyone, but especially for your mate. What can happen is that someone is confident that her thoughts have been communicated and understood. The partner is confident that the message was received loud and clear. In reality, neither event happened.

The best way to open the lines of communication is to focus your efforts on dealing with your partner the way he or she wants to be dealt with. To explain this, we'll explore the first personality area—the Introvert/Extrovert preference. This preference determines (1) how many people we are comfortable with at any one time, (2) where we do our best thinking, (3) how the brain processes information, and (4) what our verbal communication patterns are.

THE INTROVERT/EXTROVERT PREFERENCE

Introverts and Extroverts are completely opposite in what they want from discussions, social events, and the flow of discourse. They also get energized in totally different ways. Choosing the correct method makes discussions easier and often makes listening and understanding possible.

Being alone is a very different experience for Introverts and Extroverts. Introverts do their most productive thinking when alone. They're energized when they're somewhere that has a closed door or off by themselves reading a book. Extroverts, on the other hand, do their finest thinking in crowds where they can share and develop ideas with others. To Extroverts, discussing an issue is invigorating, and being around lots of people is energizing. Being alone drains them.

In the United States, about 75 percent of the people who have taken the MBTI have measured an Extroverted preference.[1] Fifty percent of relationships are a mix of Introvert and Extrovert, while the remaining 50 percent of relationships have a shared preference.

In the workplace there is about a fifty-fifty split of Introverts and Extroverts. Still, certain occupations tend to attract one type or the other. For instance, bookkeepers tend to be Introverts, and salespeople tend to be Extroverts.[2] Although both Introverts and Extroverts can be excellent communicators, they have profoundly diverse styles.

Which type are you? If you're interested, respond to the following statements.

Directions: Read each statement and check A or B next to the response, depending on which fits you better. There aren't any right, wrong, or better answers. You'll find information on scoring the test at the end.

1. If someone asks me a question, I usually:
  ☐ A) reflect for a few moments, then respond.
  ☐ B) respond immediately.

2. I prefer:
  ☐ A) being introduced to someone by another.
  ☐ B) introducing myself to someone.

3. I would rather go out:
  ☐ A) with one or two friends to a quiet restaurant.
  ☐ B) with several friends to a crowded party.

4. If I need information on a very important issue, I prefer:
  ☐ A) having someone send me information to read.
  ☐ B) discussing the topic with a knowledgeable person.

5. I prefer being with people who are:
  ☐ A) somewhat talkative.
  ☐ B) very talkative.

6. If a phone call needs to be made, I'd rather:
  ☐ A) have my spouse make it.
  ☐ B) make it myself.

7. I find my most tiring days to be:
  ☐ A) days when I meet many new people.
  ☐ B) days when I am alone.

8. If there's a long period of silence during a conversation, it's my inclination to:
  ☐ A) use it to think.
  ☐ B) fill it in.

9.   At a party, I usually:
☐ A) have deep conversations with one or two people.
☐ B) have several conversations with as many people as I can.

10.   When thinking about a new idea, I prefer:
☐ A) taking a walk someplace quiet, alone.
☐ B) talking it through with friends.

11.   After leaving a room after a spirited discussion, I'm more likely to think:
☐ A) Why didn't I say something?
☐ B) Why did I say that?

TOTALS
_____ A
_____ B

Scoring: Add the number of responses scored in the A column and the B column and put your totals at the bottom. If you scored six or more "A" responses, your preference is more likely an Introvert. If you scored six or more "B" responses, you're more likely an Extrovert.

Word and Phrases Typical to Introverts and Extroverts

Introverts	*Extroverts*
Thinking	Talking
Being alone	Being with people
Gather your thoughts	Say the first thing that comes to mind
Few good friends	Many friends
Listen	Speak

WHEN TO NEGOTIATE WITH INTROVERTS

Before you begin a discussion, set up the forum that is best for everyone. Most teenagers, through trial and error, become masters at this—learning when and where to negotiate with their parents for use of the car: (1) when their parents first get home from work; (2) during dinner; or (3) an hour after dinner. If their parents are Introverts, they know to wait until after dinner. If their parents are Extroverts, they know their greatest chance is when they get home or during dinnertime conversation.

The optimal time to talk with Introverts is after they've had a chance to be by themselves a while. Human contact and chatter tend to be exhausting for Introverts. They "charge their batteries"[3] by being by themselves. You'll have better luck negotiating with them when they're fresh and alert.

Although not all Introverts' preferences are the same, the time to meet with an Introverted mate is early in the morning, after a chance to be alone a while, or on the weekend. There should be as few people present as possible. Trying to have an important discussion with an Introvert who has just been refereeing three bickering children will make your mate ill at ease.

WHEN TO NEGOTIATE WITH EXTROVERTS

Anytime will be good for Extroverts to talk about an issue with you because they enjoy talking. Being alone is tiring to them. They charge their batteries by being around people, so if they've been alone for a while, they may need to do some small talk before they can jump in to an important issue.

THE TIME IS THE THING

Timing of interaction is critical to the success of the relationship. For instance, one partner who is an Introvert and works in a job that requires much interaction comes home to a mate who is an Extrovert and has been home alone all day. The Introvert wants time alone, and the Extrovert craves discussion and interaction. When this couple gets together at the end of a day, they are primed for conflict. Both will be run down. They need to clear their minds, but in different ways.

Even if only one partner spends the day in a way opposed to her preference, she needs to address the situation accordingly. That means that the Introvert needs to spend some time alone or the Extrovert has to spend some time at the mall.

An Introvert especially needs to be able to tell his mate that he needs "to be an Introvert" for a night or a portion of the evening. Sometimes this can cause hurt feelings in the Extroverted mate who doesn't understand the Introverted preference. The Introvert's wanting to be alone doesn't mean the Extrovert isn't loved or wanted. The Extrovert needs to find social activities apart from her mate, like visiting friends or going to crowded places. The payoff comes when the spouses get together refreshed and rejuvenated.

HOW DO YOU KNOW WHAT TYPE YOUR MATE IS?

You can find out your mate's or others' Introvert/Extrovert preference by listening and observing (or having them take the test above). No one is purely an Introvert or Extrovert, but everyone has a preference. There are times when Extroverts choose to be alone and when Introverts choose to discuss a problem with several friends.

You discover others' Introvert/Extrovert preference by asking these types of questions: "Would you like us to come by right after work, or would you like an hour to be by yourself for a while?" Extroverts will want you to come right over. Introverts will prefer you to wait a while.

Another aspect of Introvert/Extrovert preference is how people think over and respond to queries. Not surprisingly, it is very different because thought processes are not alike. Extroverts like to speak while they're thinking, and Introverts prefer thinking to themselves for about ten seconds before they speak. This difference leads to many misunderstandings that can hamper relationships.

Questions to and from Extroverts

Extroverts tend to rely on talking much more than Introverts do. When dealing with Extroverts, you'll need to have much conversation to make any interaction successful. Extroverts answer questions immediately and verbalize what they're thinking. They want to talk about solutions instead of studying them privately. Hearing an Extrovert's thoughts means you'll hear contradictory or premature views. Be careful not to interpret developing notions as conclusions.

Meg, an Introvert, and Dana, an Extrovert, are in a video rental store discussing which movie they should get.

Meg: Back to the Future is a great movie. Have you seen it yet?

Dana: No.

Meg: Let's get it.

Dana: Okay. *(A few minutes later.) The Terminator* is one of the best films I've ever seen. We should see that.

Meg stops thinking about *Back to the Future* and starts thinking about Arnold.

Meg: If you want.

Dana: Look at this movie, *The In-Laws*. Peter Falk. Alan Arkin. It's great.

Meg now starts thinking about *The In-Laws* and considers this movie. They look around a while longer. When they get to the counter, Dana is holding *Back to the Future*.

Meg: I thought you didn't want to see the movie I picked out.

Dana doesn't understand Meg's comment. When he was talking about the other movies, he was simply talking as he went around the video store. He said he wanted to see the movie Meg picked out and he meant it.

A second, and equally plausible, scenario is that Meg answers affirmatively when Dana says he wants to see *The In-laws*. Then Dana assumes that Meg wants to see it that night, he gets it, and Meg is hurt because she feels Dana doesn't take her interests in mind and isn't listening. Dana said he was listening: he clearly heard that Meg thought *The In-laws* was a good choice.

Questions to and from Introverts

Introverts tend to rely on their ability to process information in their heads, and they rely less on their verbal skills. When you have discussions with Introverts, place more importance on thinking about solutions and less on talking. Introverts will prefer to reflect on inquiries silently. They'll contemplate for about ten seconds before speaking. Interrupting Introverts while they think halts their internal deliberations. Large groups tend to be fatiguing and often overwhelming. Introverts don't express themselves best in this environment.

> The next time Meg and Dana went to the video store, Dana asked Meg which movie she'd like to see. While looking around, she saw all the boxes and thought to herself which video she wanted to rent.
> When she finished deliberating, she said, "*The Terminator.*"

The Extroverted Dana starts to speak as soon as he is asked a question. Even if he is not questioned, he'll volunteer what's going on in his brain by verbalizing his thought process. Meg waited fifteen seconds before she started speaking, and then she announced her conclusion; she didn't tell how she reached that conclusion. Introverts need time to formulate responses. *If you don't allow that time, you won't get answers.*

Introverts are doing you a favor by giving you their conclusions, but typically, they won't express how they reached their determination unless you ask them. If you feel you need to know the reasons behind an Introvert's statement, ask for clarification: "Why did you pick *The Terminator*?"

The Ineffective Way to Question Introverts

Dana, the Extrovert, is unsuccessful in communicating with Meg, the Introvert, because Meg doesn't have time to think:

> *Dana:* Meg, I'm going to be home a little late tonight, okay? There's a going-away party for a guy at the office after work.

After waiting a few seconds, assuming that Meg wouldn't mind, Dana says:

> "I'll see you around 10:00. By the way, do you want me to stop off at the store on the way home?" Unknowingly, he cut Meg off in mid-thought.
> Meg says, "We're all set, b—"

Dana keeps going:

"Great. I'll see you soon, bye."

Dana hangs up the phone confident that he and Meg success-fully communicated their feelings about his going to the party. What really happened is that Dana communicated his feelings and Meg, who wanted to contribute, said nothing. Meg had something important to say to Dana, but he missed it by cutting her off in mid-thought. When he shifted gears and asked her about bringing groceries home from the store, she halted her thoughts about going to the party and started thinking about groceries. By the time she got back to thinking about Dana's staying out, he had hung up the phone and was pleased with himself for talking issues out. He missed his last opportunity to get her true reaction.

Here's the effective way to talk things over with an Introvert like Meg.

Dana: Meg, I'm going to be home a little late tonight, okay? There's a going-away party for a guy at the office after work.

He waits before assuming there aren't any problems. Waiting is difficult for an Extrovert. (If you are one, count to ten slowly to yourself.)

Meg thinks to herself and then responds.

Meg: I don't care if you go to the party, but we have friends coming over tomorrow and we have to clean the house.

Because Dana hears the concern, he can address it.

Dana: I totally forgot about that. How about if we do this? I'll stay for a few minutes at the party and then come home and help. If I got home at seven, would that be enough time to get things done?

Meg: That's fine. See you then.

Anytime you talk with Introverts, let them speak without interruption. They speak only when a statement is well thought out and conceived.

THE EFFECTIVE WAY TO QUESTION EXTROVERTS

Drawing out the opinions of Extroverts is much easier than with Introverts, because often they'll do the work for you. They often need little encouragement, and usually just a "What do you think?" is the only tinder they'll need to start a blazing conversation.

There is one thing to watch out for. If an Extrovert who is normally quite chatty is all of a sudden quiet, then the Extrovert could be annoyed, bothered, upset, or running a temperature. Ask them what's on their mind, because there's something they want to tell you, but want to be asked.

COMMON MISCONCEPTIONS

During Conflict Without Casualty seminars, Introverts have accused Extroverts of (1) not thinking before they talk, (2) spewing verbal diarrhea, (3) being nonsensical, (4) being "fluffy," and (5) having nothing but superficial conversations. Extroverts wonder why Introverts never talk and why they don't like being around people. Extroverts report that being an Extrovert is fun while being an Introvert must be boring or sad. Before we go on, let's spend a few minutes clearing up these misconceptions.

Techniques for Extroverts

Extroverts verbalize their thoughts, so you know at any instant exactly what's on their minds. In one way they're doing you a favor, and in another way they're not. Since it's often difficult to tell the Extrovert's developing thoughts from his conclusions, you have to ask; then you'll know.

>   *Dana:* I think that we should go to an Italian restaurant tonight. Chinese food sounds good. How about if we go to Burger King?
>   *Meg:* Which is your final decision?
>   *Dana:* Chinese. Couldn't you tell?

Extroverts can help by letting others know when they're processing and when they're concluding. It's amazing how quickly arguments can happen while Extroverts are developing thoughts. This can be nipped in the bud when the Extrovert lets others know when he is thinking.

> *Dana:* Hold on. Let me think for a moment. There's no way your idea could work. [This is usually when the argument would begin.] But then again, now that I think for a moment, you have a good idea. Let's do it!

Extroverts often get into trouble—much of which will be avoided using these methods. As someone once said, "Extroverts leave a room thinking, *Why did I say that?*"

Techniques for Introverts

Introverts spend their days processing data internally, and their days are far from boring. Introverts tend to assume that if you don't ask them what they're thinking, you don't care to know. Extroverts will assume that if Introverts don't say anything, they don't have anything to say. The heartache caused by this phenomenon cannot be underestimated.

An Introverted mate may be devastated with the perception that his partner doesn't care what he says and has no interest in what he is thinking. ("She never asks.") An Extroverted mate may say that her partner doesn't want to share his life with her and that she feels distanced. ("He never talks to me.")

Fortunately, the remedy requires just a little effort by both parties. First, the Extrovert has to assume that the Introvert has important things to say and remember that just because he is not talking doesn't mean he is not thinking.

Next, the Introvert needs to remember that others do care what he says, and volunteer what's on his mind without prompting. At first, this seems difficult for him to do. But it becomes easier with practice. An Introvert often leaves a room thinking, *I can't believe I didn't say anything.*

Another phenomenon is common to Introverts: filtering. Sometimes Introverts, in the zeal to speak only about things that are well thought out, turn up their filter too high. For instance, something could be bothering them, but they wait so long to make sure, the event is forgotten. Or else they opt for silence instead of conversation.

If this is the case for you, turn down the filter, and begin sharing your introspections sooner than you might think is appropriate. Your partner will be happy you did.

Finally, there's nothing sad about being an Introvert. As long as Introverts are receiving stimulation of one sort or another, they're perfectly content.

INTROVERT/EXTROVERT COMBINATIONS

In any couple there are three possible combinations of Introvert/Extrovert preferences: (1) two Extroverts, (2) two Introverts, and (3) a combination of Extrovert and Introvert. Each case has its strengths and weaknesses, but all combinations can work. Here's how.

Two Extroverts

Strengths. Two Extroverts will have lively conversations, and they tend to be very sociable. Each partner will tend to crave the other's company.

Liabilities. There will be two good talkers but not necessarily any good listeners. Ideas taken prematurely can start controversies like a wildfire out of control. Debating for a victory can replace understanding for solutions during conflicts.

Remedy. Learn to let each other talk. One partner doesn't talk until the other partner says he or she has nothing more to say. Ask which part of a statement was the developing thought and which was the conclusion. If the issue at hand is volatile, both parties could write their concerns, then swap what they wrote with no commenting until both have finished reading.

Two Introverts

Strengths. Both will tend to be good listeners. Introverts find discussing subjects with Extroverts difficult because they often feel they can't get a word in. Since statements are well thought out, tête-à-têtes tend to be interesting and insightful.

Liabilities. Both parties may be good listeners, but often there's no talking to listen to. The biggest complaint of two Introverts is that things are too quiet.

Remedy. If things are too quiet, both partners need to turn down the filter and not wait for prompting to begin a conversation. Also, if you're looking for fodder for discussions, find areas of common interest, like movies or TV or books, and talk about them. Or you could get a pet, share a hobby, or take a course. If both like reading, read aloud to each other every now and then.

Introvert/Extrovert

Strengths. An Introvert and an Extrovert complement each other well, especially when they use Conflict Without Casualty techniques. An Introvert gets some added sociability and chatter, while an Extrovert learns the value of having a deeper relationship.

Liabilities. If partners don't use Conflict Without Casualty techniques, one or both can feel stifled or abandoned.

Remedy. Use the Conflict Without Casualty techniques in this chapter.

GENERAL CONFLICT WITHOUT CASUALTY TECHNIQUES WITH INTROVERTS AND EXTROVERTS

When using Conflict Without Casualty techniques, remember that Extroverts enjoy discussions and like being in large groups, and they will speak as they think. They'll enjoy parties and have more fun as the evening wears on.

Introverts prefer being by themselves or with one or a few close friends. They spend time thinking about what they say and verbalize only their conclusions. Introverts like parties, too, but being with a number of people they don't know well is very draining to them. According to Keirsey and Bates, "It's not that Introverts are party poopers, it's they're pooped by the party."[4] (It's interesting to watch Introverts and Extroverts at parties. The Introverts will have a few long talks; Extroverts will work the crowd. Extroverts will make small talk with as many people as they can.)

Now we're going to see how the Introvert/Extrovert preference is used in practice. Communication between partners involves knowing about Introvert/Extrovert preferences and some additional strategies.

Step 1: Get Everyone Involved

Anytime several people are involved in a discussion, there are likely to be some who try to dominate the conversation and others who don't want to speak very much. This is a prescription for disaster in a relationship. Solutions negotiated without addressing the concerns of each member of the couple will get no support or lukewarm support later on.

A common negotiating exercise has two parts. The first part is to have several participants negotiate a single group decision. After the group returns with a decision, the second part begins. Each participant rates feelings about the negotiation experience by writing on a piece of paper, on a scale from one to ten, two things: (1) how the decision reflects personal feelings on the subject, and (2) how much each is going to support the group in implementing the plan. Participants also note how much involvement they had during the negotiation.

The ones who contributed their thoughts during the negotiation rate both categories high, usually eight or higher. This is true even if the final solution was different from the solution they endorsed.

The ones who didn't participate in the negotiation rate both categories low, usually four or lower. This is true even when the solution was similar to one they endorsed.

When a plan goes awry, those who dominated the discussion will bang their heads against the wall and say, "I asked you what you felt, and you didn't say anything."

The silent members will say, "You never asked what I thought, so I assumed that you didn't care" (between head bangs).

After everyone takes some aspirin and begins using Conflict Without Casualty techniques, participants will have much more success.

An exercise used in counseling is effective in relationship negotiations. The idea is that one doesn't respond to a concern until he can suitably repeat that concern back to his partner. Not surprisingly, especially with deep-seated concerns, it takes a few tries to convince the other person you understand his position.

Step 2: Show Appreciation for Positions

We all want to feel that our ideas and values have merit. We cherish being understood, and we feel good about the folks we talk to when they react positively to us while they listen. We tend to like people who listen to us and to dislike or feel neutral to the ones who don't.

You need to reward your mate by showing that you enjoy listening and you really appreciate what your mate is saying. That's different from agreeing, but when you agree with your mate, appreciation will flow naturally.

Although you're likely to agree with your mate on most subjects, you won't always have that luxury. Let's face it. Committed relationships beyond the age of nineteen aren't always a love-in where everybody is praising everybody else's virtues. For Conflict Without Casualty to work, you need appreciation of, not agreement with, your partner's views.

To have a successful discussion, you do not have to agree with your partner. (Elwood P. Dowd in Mary Chase's *Harvey*, immortalized by the invisible rabbit-seeing Jimmy Stewart, said, "An element of conflict in any discussion is a good thing. It means everybody is taking part and nobody is left out. I like that.")[5] *You must,* however, appreciate your partner's position. Here are examples of the reactions you can expect to appreciation and nonappreciation. First is the appreciative mate.

Appreciation: I understand how important you feel it is to have our children in a private grammar school. I feel, however, that until they are ready for high school, the public school in our town is just as excellent as the private school.

Reaction: I'm glad you listened to me, though you have a different conclusion. Now I'm going to listen to you too.

Next is the nonappreciative negotiator.

Nonappreciation: Can't you see that paying a snowplow thirty-five dollars to clear the driveway is like flushing money down the toilet?

Reaction: If you weren't such a pompous tightwad, maybe I'd listen to you.

When people feel others don't acknowledge the merit in what they're saying, the usual outcomes are attacking and escalating the animosity or avoiding the aggressor and halting the discussion.

If you agree with a position, fine. If you're the type of person who finds it easy to understand and accept another's position, that will promote discussions. If you're having trouble understanding a viewpoint that is contrary to yours, just ask and empathize.

Asking and empathizing tell your loved one that you don't understand, but you want to understand. All but the most difficult people will work as hard at explaining as you are at listening. The longer the process goes on, the narrower the misunderstanding gaps become.

THERE ARE OTHER DIMENSIONS TOO

In addition to the Introvert/Extrovert preference in this chapter, there are three other preferences. Next, we will look at the Sensing/Intuitive preference. It measures how much detail we like and how we develop concerns.

Keeping Conflict from Happening

CHAPTER FOUR

Conflict Without Casualty Provides an Ounce of Prevention

This chapter focuses on outlooks and why we and our mates react to situations very differently. A significant part of Conflict Without Casualty is keeping conflicts from occurring by nipping controversy in the bud. Perceptions alone can strengthen or destroy relationships.

The unchecked second personality area, the Sensing/Intuitive preference, is the breeding ground for hostility, and this preference determines to a great extent how we interpret the behavior of others. The Sensing/Intuitive preference is a major cause of marital dissatisfaction in issues like housekeeping, money, sex, appearance, and long-term planning. It can act like a wedge, driving partners apart. When partners use this difference to their advantage, however, it will act as a bonding force, making the couple stronger.

Sensing types use their five senses and their ability to calculate to appreciate their environment and form judgments. They're very detail oriented and notice everything. Aggravations brew when their senses are violated. They'll insist on a neat house, a well-balanced checkbook, practical thinking, and physically pleasing sensations. Sensing types tend to see Intuitive mates as having their heads in the clouds.

Intuitive types thrive on looking at possibilities, and they prefer discussing the big picture. They want to consider future plans and want to know why a subject is important before chewing into it. They tend not to notice or care about details. And they piece together facts to draw conclusions. The problem is that during controversies, Intuitives tend to think their Sensing mates are narrow-minded, inflexible, and picky.

Sensing types and Intuitive types tend to date, and later marry, because they complement each other. Sensing types like the creativity of Intuitives, and Intuitives like the stability of Sensing types. During conflicts, each can feel that he or she is getting too much of a good thing, or that the partner is being stubborn and unresponsive.

Instead of trying to change your mate, you can capitalize on the strengths as a couple and invent options to make everyone a winner. For instance, instead of arguing about the proper method to attack household jobs, divide chores according to type. The Intuitive type does less-detailed cleaning, like loading the dishwasher and vacuuming. The Sensing type does detailed cleaning, like dusting, making the bed, and cleaning the crumbs under the toaster. This strategy allows you and your mate to avoid a battle of wills, and it makes the most of personal preferences.

The Introvert/Extrovert preference, discussed in the last chapter, helps with verbal communication and thinking patterns. The Sensing/Intuitive preference takes communication a step farther.

THE SENSING/INTUITIVE PREFERENCE

Before delving into this preference, respond to the statements below. Next, complete the brief exercise. We use this in seminars, and the attendees find it very helpful. First, here's the test.

Directions: Read each statement and check A or B next to the response, depending on which fits you better. There aren't any right, wrong, or better answers. You'll find information on scoring the test at the end.

1. **When understanding a new concept, I first want:**
    ☐ A) details.
    ☐ B) an overview.

2. **When I am learning a new concept, a lot of details first:**
    ☐ A) are important.
    ☐ B) are confusing.

3. **When describing something, I usually:**
   ☐ A) describe it literally.
   ☐ B) describe it conceptually.

4. **I clean a mess that can't be seen:**
   ☐ A) as often as I can.
   ☐ B) once in a while.

5. **I usually:**
   ☐ A) notice little things before others do.
   ☐ B) have others point little things out to me.

6. **If I were to get a new TV, I would buy:**
   ☐ A) tried and true.
   ☐ B) the latest and greatest.

7. **My goal for handling my checkbook is:**
   ☐ A) to balance it to the penny.
   ☐ B) to not bounce checks.

8. **I enjoy music for:**
   ☐ A) its beat and melody.
   ☐ B) the meaning of the lyrics.

9. **Others would describe me as having:**
   ☐ A) my feet on the ground.
   ☐ B) my head in the clouds.

10. **As far as rules and procedures are concerned:**
    ☐ A) I know what they are and I either always keep them or never keep them.
    ☐ B) I think of as many solutions to the problem as possible, despite the established rules.

11. **If there was a pile of dirty dishes in the sink before I went to bed, I would:**
    ☐ A) have trouble sleeping.
    ☐ B) not give it a second thought.

TOTALS

———— A

———— B

Scoring: Add the number of responses scored in the A column and the B column and put your totals at the bottom. If you scored six or more "A" responses, your preference is more likely Sensing. If you scored six or more "B" responses, you're more likely Intuitive.

Here's a list of words and phrases that typify how Sensing and Intuitive types think and look at the world. Remember that we have a little of each type in us, and a preference is the type that we tend to find more natural and comfortable.

Words and Phrases Typical of Sensing and Intuitive Types

Sensing	*Intuitive*
Orderly	Free-flowing
Facts	Big picture
Here and now	Theory
Practical	Ideas
Cautious	Possibilities
Problems that could arise	Potential, not problems
Deal with what we have	Associations
Glass half empty	Glass half full
Let's be realistic	Simplify a problem
Worry about the details now	Worry about the details later

Sensing types and Intuitives see the world very differently. When you talk things over, know your partner's type, so you can adjust the words you use and what you say.

THE SENSING/INTUITIVE EXERCISE

This exercise demonstrates the Sensing/Intuitive preference. It takes only a few minutes, and you'll probably find it fun. Ask your partner to do it too. (Don't peek at each other's list because it will influence the results.) Put an apple on the table. Then list all the words that come to mind in describing the apple. After you're finished, read the lists that seminar members came up with. Compare your list.

Sensates use the five senses to describe the apple, while Intuitives describe the concept of apple. Typical lists look like the following:

Sensing	*Intuitive*
Shiny	Good
Red	Teacher
Has a stem	Computers
Seeds	Grandmother's house
Nutritious	Adam and Eve
Tastes good	Sin and temptation
Good for you	Garden of Eden
Round	Johnny Appleseed
	New York City
	Bobbing for apples
	Halloween
	Vitamin A
	Washington State

Sensing types will tell you how it looks, feels, and tastes and what it sounds like when you bite into it. (Sensing types handle the apple and eat it.) They use their five senses and their calculating ability to gain or give information on ideas, objects, or events. Their lists tend to give facts about the apple and aspects of the apple that can be observed. Their lists are short because there's only so much to be said about facts and observable traits.

Intuitives like concepts. They talk and think about possibilities. The Intuitive list is very different from the Sensing list in that it contains general information and associations about the apple. Intuitives generally never pick up the apple or comment that a particular apple is red. How long can an Intuitive's list be? At one seminar, the Intuitive group participants compiled their lists for about two hours. They came up with sixty-four pages of associations, and they could have filled more.

GENERAL CONFLICT WITHOUT CASUALTY
TECHNIQUES WITH SENSING
AND INTUITIVE TYPES

No type is better or worse, but both types are very different. It shouldn't be a big stretch to figure out that if we look at an apple very differently, we perceive all aspects of life differently too. Let's consider some techniques to use with Sensing and Intuitive types.

Step 1: Broach Ideas to Just Think About

Now that we have looked at the difference between Sensing and Intuitive types, let's look at a few of the steps you'll use to understand and begin to develop solutions to concerns that you and your mate will have.

Sometimes you don't want to bring up concerns and insist on solutions in the same conversation. Not seeking an immediate solution doesn't mean you're avoiding conflict, and it can often be a tactical advantage. This is especially true if an immediate solution isn't needed, which is almost always the case.

Separating the expression of concerns from the beginning of options will take advantage of differences of types because the solutions will be strong. If the type is the same, it will keep you from reinforcing biases, which can happen if everyone looks at an issue in the same way.

Reinforcing biases happens, for instance, when two Intuitives are creative in inventing options, but neglect to find one that is practical. It also happens when Sensing types give up on a problem too soon because brainstorming isn't their strength.

Let's take a look at when to use each strategy.

Bringing Up Concerns

Sometimes you'll want to bring up concerns and ask your partner to think about solutions. Of course, the Introvert/Extrovert preference mixes with the Sensing/Intuitive preference. An Introverted Sensing type will want to internally debate details, while an Extroverted Intuitive type will want to talk about the theory.

Let's investigate how the four types we've discussed so far bring up concerns.

An Introvert does best when allowed to contemplate situations. If you and your partner are an Introvert/Extrovert mix, the Introvert will find it difficult to jump into inventing options with the Extrovert because the Extrovert throws out undeveloped ideas and quickly dismisses them.

Give the Introvert thinking time, and then begin the conversation to air views.

The Extrovert blurts out the first idea that comes to mind, which may or may not be the best idea. This tendency could create unnecessary tension between the Extrovert and the Introvert, or it could put the Extrovert in the position of feeling he or she has to defend a statement that is still developing. An Extrovert does the best thinking when permitted to talk a problem through, so take that into account.

If both you and your partner are Extroverts, set the ground rules to just discuss the issues but not come to any conclusion. Waiting a while is good for sensitive topics because both of you can be introspective and think about what you're going to say.

Sensing types tend to be good at coming up with a practical solution, but the flip side is that they also tend to self-filter their creative ideas. Giving a Sensate partner time to ponder the solution helps avoid the knee-jerk reactions that occur when the Sensate focuses on all the details of what could go wrong.

Intuitives will be great at coming up with creative options, but the options they come up with initially may not be practical. The ideas may be so outlandish that you (especially if you're a Sensate) may lose faith that any solution of your Intuitive partner would be feasible. Allow time so the Intuitive may analyze different ways the concerns could be met that would have a high probability of working.

Conflict Resolution Style

Separating bringing up concerns from inventing options will help with different conflict resolution styles too. Perhaps your partner is inclined to avoid conflict or seek a one-sided win. To encourage your partner to think about solutions that benefit everyone, you may want to say, "I have some concerns. Let's think about them for a while, and we can both come up with ways that my concerns and any concerns you have can be met. I'm sure we can come up with something that's good for both of us." This strategy gives the conflict avoider permission to confront the problem. It also gives the person who is adversarial time to filter through adversarial ideas and start the collaborative process.

Step 2: Deflect Unproductive Behavior

Let's say your partner does something unproductive while the two of you are solving a conflict. You have the option of letting the conversation get off track or deflecting the behavior. Unproductive behavior can take many forms: ridiculing, ignoring, threatening, laughing at, mimicking, and/or making light of you or your concerns. Deflection can take lots of self-control.

Deflecting the behavior while the conflict is ongoing is different from being a doormat. Afterward, you definitely want to mention to your partner that you felt hurt when you were ridiculed or demeaned in any way, as in the following scenario:

Marie: Last weekend, on the way to the movies, we were discussing which movie to watch. Making me sound like a shrieking fishwife made me feel bad.

Jack: I know. I wanted to see *Bikini-Clad Babes Crash Cars and Blow Up Buildings* so much, I would do anything to see it. I acted like a jerk to pressure you into seeing it. I'm sorry.

This exchange is a big improvement for Jack and Marie. Before they had conflict resolution training, this would happen:

Marie: I want to see *Terminally Ill People Find Happiness*.

Jack: I want to see *Bikini-Clad Babes Crash Cars and Blow Up Buildings*.

Marie: I want to see my movie.

Jack: [He speaks in a derogatory imitation.] I want to see my movie.

Marie: Forget it. Take me home. I don't feel well.

Both would lose. No one would see a movie, and both would feel bad, which is contrary to the goal of going on a date.

When you deflect behavior, you ignore it. Don't give the abusive party the satisfaction of a response of any kind. Instead, dauntlessly focus on your partner's concerns and bring up your concerns.

> *Marie:* What are some ways that we could see your movie and my movie?
>
> *Jack:* That's impossible.
>
> *Marie:* Why don't we see my movie at 7:00, see your movie at 9:30, and go out afterward?
>
> *Jack:* That sounds pretty decadent.
>
> *Marie:* We're married. We're allowed to be decadent.

Step 3: Say What's Important to You

After laying out the concerns on the table, prioritize what's most important to you, as I mentioned in chapter 2.

Step 4: Ask Sincere Questions

Until you and your partner become adept at understanding and verbalizing your concerns, you'll need to use techniques to bring out the concerns. Many times, people's concerns are not well-developed thoughts but feelings. The way to bridge the gap between feelings and workable concerns is to ask questions.

A sincere question is one that you truly don't know the answer to. A rule in negotiations is that sincere questions are always appropriate. A corollary to that principle is that sincere questions will prompt sincere responses.

Insincere questions, on the other hand, are questions you know the answer to or ones you use to verbally manipulate, attack, or belittle the person you're asking the question of. Lawyers learn in law school to never ask a question they don't know the answer to. They also learn that making adversaries appear brainless and themselves appear smart wins points with clients.

Couples can get trapped into playing the Cross Examination game, which I'll talk about in chapter 7. For now, know that people who need to appear clever at others' expense are behaving in a damaging and ineffective way.

COPING WITH AN EXTREME PERSONALITY

When you're dealing with an extreme personality type, recognize that strong types are trying to be helpful, not difficult. This is sometimes hard to do while you're pulling your hair out. For example, tell your supreme Sensate partner that you appreciate the attention to detail, but that level of detail is not necessary at this time.

Nick and Carol have been married for two years. Carol is a Sensing type, and Nick is an Intuitive. Carol has always paid the bills, and Nick thinks she does a great job.

They decided that they wanted to save for a house and would keep to a strict budget for two years so they would have the down payment and closing costs. They decided that they would go over all of their expenses each Sunday night.

Carol would go over each expenditure in the ledger and spend up to ten minutes fixing discrepancies. Nick didn't care about the seventy-nine cents that they spent for milk on Thursday. He just wanted to know that miscellaneous expenses for the week were fifteen dollars.

Nick found the budget conversation frustrating and would quickly tune Carol out when she started getting too detailed for him.

They decided that she would go over the figures and let him know the conclusions. Also, she would collapse categories to a few main items like food, entertainment, and rent so he could see the big picture.

If they were overspending in one area, Nick would look at the numbers and find big items or a trend causing the problem.

Perhaps your partner is an intense Intuitive. Say that you appreciate the creativity and the concern with future problems but that the focus of the discussion needs to be the problem at hand: "I love your creativity, and I definitely want to think about your idea. For now, let's put blinders on so that we can focus on this concern."

Of course, Sensates and Intuitives see most things differently. It's not surprising they want things explained in various ways too.

EXPLAIN IT TO ME

So that your concerns will be understood, you must phrase them in a way compatible with the type of person you're communicating with. When you and your partner are different types, you have to be sensitive to the fact that your mate may have a different learning style. When you explain your concerns about the car or the checkbook, you need to be careful.

Rich is a Sensing type, and Ginny is an Intuitive. They bought a new car with antilock brakes. In case of a sudden stop, the manual dictates that the brakes not be pumped. Rich followed the directions of the manual and experienced the car coming to a hard stop. He didn't question the manual since it was his nature to follow directions.

Ginny didn't trust the manual. She knew how the brakes on their old car worked, and she still pumped the brakes for fear of their locking up. She figured that the old way of pumping brakes would work at least as well with the new technology. Ginny needed to know the theory of antilock brakes before she'd feel comfortable using them.

Rick called a mechanic they know and asked him why the manual said not to pump the brakes. He found out that a computer inside the car pumped the brakes several times a second, much faster than a person could. If, during an emergency, you pump the brakes, it will confuse the computer, and the car will stop less quickly and with less control.

After knowing the theory, Ginny would slam her foot on the brakes and not pump them because she knew it was the best course of action.

In this chapter, we looked at how couples generate concerns and look at situations. In the next chapter, we'll look at the emotional aspect of relationships using the Thinking/Feeling preference.

How We Express Love, Develop Concerns, and Relate to Others

CHAPTER FIVE

Conflict Without Casualty Helps Couples Get Interpersonal

Isaac Newton said, "For every action, there is an equal and opposite reaction." That holds true for relationships as well as for physics. This chapter focuses on what we get emotional about, how we internalize and express these sentiments, what we expect of our mates as we emote, and how to channel all these feelings positively. This chapter covers the very personal interpersonal relations partners have with each other, important subjects like development and expression of emotion, the effective way to address concerns, and the way in which harmony, criticism, logic, self-improvement, conflict resolution, and sexuality intertwine in relationships.

The third Conflict Without Casualty area, the Thinking/Feeling preference, explains the dynamics of a relationship in several ways. The first is emotional, that is, how we act and interact, process information, and receive and express emotion, both physically and verbally. The second way the Thinking/Feeling preference is important is that it determines how we develop concerns and how others can satisfy them. We'll cover the emotional side first and then get into handling concerns and conflicting concerns later on in the chapter.

But before we go any farther, you need to know more about the two types.

THE THINKING/FEELING PREFERENCE

Thinking types view people and things analytically and objectively. Feeling types view people and things personally and emotionally. While Thinking types tend to find it easy to think of groups impersonally, feeling types view groups as a collection of individuals. Feeling types want to improve people's lives, while Thinking types are motivated by logic.

If you're interested in ascertaining your type, take the following test.

Directions: Read each statement and check A or B next to the response, depending on which fits you better. There aren't any right, wrong, or better answers. You'll find information on scoring the test at the end.

1. **If I make a decision, I will be swayed by:**
   ☐ A) how I'm sure it will turn out.
   ☐ B) how I hope it will turn out.

2. **If I were buying something for someone else, I'd be concerned:**
   ☐ A) that I was buying the right thing.
   ☐ B) that the person would like it.

3. **I like dealing with people who are:**
   ☐ A) predictable.
   ☐ B) nice.

4. **When I buy something, I'm more concerned with:**
   ☐ A) its cost.
   ☐ B) how much people will like it.

5. **When I think about a certain class of people, I tend to think of them in terms of:**
   ☐ A) group characteristics.
   ☐ B) individual differences.

6. **If I'm at a family gathering and two people are arguing, I:**
   ☐ A) assume that interpersonal conflict is unavoidable.
   ☐ B) feel uncomfortable that there is disharmony.

7. **If I saw a stray cat that was hungry, but my house was a little small for a pet, I would:**
   ☐ A) take the cat in to an animal shelter.
   ☐ B) take the cat in.

8. **If someone complained about my family, I would:**
   ☐ A) not take it personally.
   ☐ B) take it personally.

9. **After trying to make a disgruntled person happy, with no luck, I would:**
   ☐ A) give up.
   ☐ B) keep trying until I was successful.

10. **My best buying decisions were made:**
    ☐ A) rationally and precisely.
    ☐ B) emotionally.

11. **After I am emotional:**
    ☐ A) I often regret it.
    ☐ B) I feel relieved.

TOTALS

_____ A
_____ B

Scoring: Add the number of responses scored in the A column and the B column, and put your totals at the bottom. If you scored six or more "A" responses, your preference is more likely a Thinking type. If you scored six or more "B" responses, you're more likely a Feeling type.

Here's a list of words and phrases that typify how Thinking and Feeling types think and look at the world.

Words and Phrases Typical of Thinking and Feeling Types

Thinking	*Feeling*
Fair	Just
Impartial	Good
Practical	Harmony

Words and Phrases Typical of Thinking and Feeling Types—*Cont'd*

Thinking	*Feeling*
Right	Happy
Makes sense	Passionate
Take your medicine,	Life's too
it's good for you	short
Rational	Emotions
Logical	Reasonable
Who's right	What went wrong

Thinking types look at situations logically and unemotionally. *Star Trek*'s Mr. Spock is the stereotypical Thinking type. (For those of you who aren't Trekkies, Mr. Spock is from the planet Vulcan. The Vulcans base their lives purely on logic, and they have no emotions.) Thinking types have feelings, but they would never characterize themselves as being overly sentimental. Instead, they see themselves as having the appropriate amount of sentimentality for any given occasion. Thinking types are the anchor of reason in a sea of emotion.

Feeling types are likely to attach meaning and emotion to as many parts of their lives as they can. Stereotypical Feeling types are the people who have thirty stray cats living with them. Feeling types use as much logic and analytical reasoning as they feel the situation requires. They relish warmth, meaningful relationships, and harmony. Feeling types are the guiding current in a sea of indifference.

As we have seen with the other preferences, no one is a pure type (either all Thinking or all Feeling). We have a little of both in our makeup.

Here's an example of a Thinking type and a Feeling type in action:

A couple's baby is vomiting in the middle of the night. The Feeling type will comfort the baby, and the Thinking type will call the doctor to see if the sickness is serious enough to take her to the hospital.

In this situation the Feeling type did a great job of comforting the baby, but if the baby were acutely ill, precious minutes would have been lost. (Of course, the Feeling type assumed the baby had a virus or bad mushed up bananas.)

The Thinking type suspected the baby had the flu but wasn't willing to risk it. Even though the baby was screaming, the Thinking type felt that averting a catastrophe by making a call was more important than comforting a little crying. (The Thinking type assumed the baby would be okay eventually.)

Once again, no type is better, and each type complements the other nicely. In the example, having both a Thinking type and a Feeling type in the family meant that correct medical information was obtained and the baby was comforted.

Stereotypical thinking may make people believe that all women are Feeling types and all men are Thinking types. Let's look at the facts as far as gender is concerned.

THINKING/FEELING TYPES AND GENDER

In the United States, men are socialized to be Thinking types, and women are socialized to be Feeling types. The reality is that 60 percent of women score Feeling and 40 percent score Thinking. For men, it's just about the opposite, 60 percent score Thinking and 40 percent score Feeling. So much for stereotypes!

These figures blow the myth that all women are Feeling types and are concerned with emotional needs, and that all men are Thinking types and are concerned with problem solving and logical analysis. Some men feel bad about being Feeling types because they believe emotions are not manly. Some women who are Thinking types believe they are too coldhearted.

You can't change the type that God dealt you. All types are equally good and have strength and value. In the example above of the sick child, if the Thinking type was a woman calling the doctor, that wouldn't be coldhearted; it would be loving in a different way.

HOW TO KNOW WHETHER SOMEONE IS A THINKING OR FEELING TYPE

How can you tell if someone is a Thinking or Feeling type? By listening and observing.

If she says things like, "It's the lesser of two evils," "I want it to be efficient," "Let's look at this from afar," or "If they don't like it, too bad!" she is a Thinking type.

If he says, "I want everybody to be happy," "I don't like all the tension," "Let's imagine how they feel," he is a Feeling type.

Next, we'll look at several aspects of being a Thinking or Feeling type.

HOW WE EXPRESS LOVE

The first major difference in Thinking and Feeling types is the way love is expressed. A person may wake up one day with the horrible feeling that his partner doesn't love him anymore. He feels lonely and abandoned, and even though his partner tells him that nothing could be farther from the truth, he doesn't believe it. The Thinking/Feeling preference explains how easily it can happen in relationships.

As we know, we tend to deal with others the way we want to be dealt with. A natural tendency is to express love to others the way we want others to express love to us. That sounds so good. But that works only with people who share our personality preferences.

Perceptions about how your spouse feels about you or the depth of his or her love are based on receiving or not receiving the type of affection you would like. The remedy is usually simple: replace feeling hurt with knowing that your mate is trying to say, "I love you," in his or her own way. As you'll see, Thinking types and Feeling types are very different in how they express all emotions, including love.

A Thinking type expresses love by doing things for his mate, for instance, making a favorite meal. A Feeling type expresses love by sharing emotions, for instance, expressing her feelings with words and touch.

Imagine this scenario:

Collin prepares his wife's favorite meal, hoping to convey how much he loves her. He spent all afternoon shopping in the supermarket, setting the table, and putting dinner in the oven. All he could think was how much he loved Tricia. And he was looking forward to spending time with her as they ate.

Tricia, a Feeling type, comes home and wraps her arms around him and says, "I thought about you today." Collin is so busy with the mashed potatoes that he doesn't have a hand free to hug her. He says, "Hi, Trish."

Tricia presumes that Collin doesn't care about being thought of and can't take two seconds from making his stupid mashed potatoes to hug her. She concludes he cares more about the roast beef than her emotional needs. Then she figures that if he doesn't care about her feelings, he doesn't really care about her.

After spending all afternoon making dinner, Collin is surprised that Tricia doesn't acknowledge the effort or express thanks. Collin reasons that she doesn't appreciate the things he does for her; therefore, she doesn't appreciate him.

After dinner, both stew for a while and go to bed with damaged egos, feeling hurt and unappreciated. They sleep as far apart from each other as they can.

In reality, each partner cares passionately about the other but expresses love differently. Awareness of how people express love and emotion remedies the problem. Here's how Tricia and Collin relate to each other using Conflict Without Casualty:

> When Tricia gets home, she tells Collin, "You were on my mind all day."
>
> Collin says, "I thought about you, too, when I was in the supermarket. Next thing you know I'm making roast beef. I hope you like it. I'd give you a big hug, but my hands are covered with mashed potatoes."
>
> Tricia responds, "I really appreciate your going to all this work for me. I feel so special. Hug me—mashed potatoes and all."

Using Conflict Without Casualty, they know how they want love expressed and how the partner does too. The passion they feel for each other is the same in both scenarios, but in the first, that passion is diverted into hurt feelings and directed inward. In the second, using Conflict Without Casualty, that same love is expressed in ways attuned to their types. Instead of going to bed hurt and bewildered, they go to bed feeling loved.

When they are dating, both people usually go to great lengths to please. Thinking types are pampered with thoughtful acts. Feeling types are frequently greeted with loving gestures and sentiments.

After two people get married, there's a strong tendency to get caught up in the struggles of daily life: commuting to work, mowing the lawn, driving the kids to soccer practice. The attention that nourished the Thinking and Feeling types during dating and the newlywed stage starts to decrease or even disappear.

Loving someone the way she wants to be loved doesn't take a lot of time or effort. The object is to constantly be mindful that this is an important aspect of life, and you'll see that the little things add up and make life more pleasant for both of you.

THINKING/FEELING TYPES AND SEXUALITY

Through sexual relations, including making love, spouses express emotions, feel wanted and giving, and feel sensuous and sensual pleasure. Although the Thinking/Feeling preference, like any one psychological theory, doesn't completely explain sexual dynamics, it does illuminate many aspects of sexuality in marriage.

Thinking types and Feeling types view physical intimacy far differently. Since Feeling types strive for meaning in their lives, they want intimate acts to be meaningful too. Feeling types want to make the people they love happy, and sex is a great avenue for that. Also, Feeling types tend to meld sex and love together, and they will find it difficult to separate the two.

Thinking types tend to view sex as the sharing and communication avenue that Feeling types do, but they also see it as a stress release and recreation.

The Thinking/Feeling preference determines how we express love as well as how we react when we are upset or face conflict.

GENERAL CONFLICT WITHOUT CASUALTY TECHNIQUES WITH THINKING AND FEELING TYPES—HOW CONCERNS ARE DEVELOPED

Thinking types and Feeling types view conflict completely differently. Both types develop concerns and approach conflicts in characteristic ways.

Because Thinking types tend to look at the world matter-of-factly, they can sometimes be unaware of the sea of emotion around them. When Feeling types have concerns, Thinking types want to know examples of what they did that upset them. They are not being defensive or obtrusive; they want sample data so they can better understand the concerns. When Feeling types are upset, they want empathy. They find it irrelevant to give examples because the fact that they're upset is the issue. Feeling types may become resentful at having to provide "proof," and they will say things like, "I don't want to justify the way I feel."

Once examples are given, a Thinking type may say that the concern is perfectly valid, or he may offer an explanation. A Thinking type is constantly reasoning before, during, and after a problem crops up or an action is taken. He wants to share his thought process with you. He seeks affirmation that the thought process was unflawed, even if the result was. Don't battle him. Instead, let him know that his reasoning was perfect, or you understand why he took such an action. Still, the expected result was not attained, or there is more data to put into the thought process. It may take concentration at times, but remember that a Thinking type is not trying to be difficult.

Steve is a Thinking type, and Rebecca is a Feeling type. This is what can happen:

Rebecca: Steve, I'm upset about your leaving the car with no gas in it. You do it all the time. I almost ran out of gas as I drove the kids to school, and it was cold outside.
Steve: I didn't leave you in the lurch. And I don't do it all the time.
Rebecca: Forget it, obviously you don't want to talk.
Steve: Fine.

They're now angry with each other. Next, they try their conversation, keeping type in mind.

Steve: It must have been stressful taking the kids to school and being worried about being stranded in the cold. I'll try to be more careful to leave enough gas in the car. I'm trying to understand something. I don't remember your ever running out of gas.
Rebecca: I did last year.

Steve: That was when the snowstorm knocked power out and the gas stations were closed, wasn't it? You were able to start again because I put a gas can in the trunk. [Steve is explaining why he feels that running out of gas is, in his mind, not an issue.] I knew the gas was low this morning, but I thought you'd use the emergency credit card in the glove compartment.

Rebecca: I forgot it was there.

Steve: The only reason the gas was low this morning was that I was running late so I wouldn't miss the kids' soccer game. I looked at the gauge and it seemed to me that you had enough to get to a station.

Rebecca: You're right. Next time, let me know before I leave the house, so I don't panic.

Steve: Okay. You're right. I was running late and didn't take the time to call you. If that happens again, I'll let you know.

Instead of Steve feeling bad about being thought of as irresponsible, all of his efforts for making contingency plans are acknowledged. With that being done, he is willing to admit that he didn't think there was an emergency, and that it would be easy for Rebecca to assume that the extra gas and credit card were there only in the winter.

Rebecca is willing to acknowledge that Steve did care about her concerns, but that communication was the issue, not irresponsibility. Finally, they have set up a structure so that this problem doesn't occur in the future.

Step 1: Recognize the Preferred Approach to Problems

When presented with a problem, a Thinking type immediately wants to problem solve. A Feeling type doesn't want solutions immediately (or sometimes at all); she wants someone to listen to her and empathize.

Rebecca: I have this coworker who is a big pain.

Steve: Tell me about it.

Rebecca: Well, she's constantly watching the clock, like she's a hall monitor. She'll say things like, "You're two minutes late from your break," or "I thought lunchtime was an hour." My boss doesn't care if I'm a little late because she knows that I get to work early on many days.

Steve: [His natural reaction is to begin to problem solve and figure some way of stopping the unwanted behavior of the coworker. He knows that Rebecca doesn't want solutions now; she wants empathy.] It must be hard working with the clock police.

Rebecca: Oh, it is.

After you know others' preferred approach, remind yourself—if your preferred way is different—to understand where your love is coming from.

Step 2: Respect the Other's Sensitivities

Thinking types tend not to care about what people—especially people they don't know—think about their actions. Because they're concerned with harmony, Feeling types tend to worry about being yelled at, and they are ever aware of what people think. Being yelled at is one of Feeling types' greatest worries. Thinking and Feeling types differ in their perception of what being yelled at is and means.

When Larry, a Feeling type, and Terry, a Thinking type, were in couples' therapy, Larry complained that Terry constantly yelled at him. Terry objected and said that she never yelled at him. I asked Larry if he could provide some examples.

He said, "Well, like last Sunday when I was making you breakfast, you yelled at me."

Terry immediately shouted, "I did not!"

Larry said, "When I was making you pancakes, you came into the kitchen and said, 'You shouldn't use a metal spatula on Silverstone because it will scratch.'"

"That's yelling?" she said as she threw up her arms.

"Yes, I was very hurt, and you ruined my whole day off."

Terry ruined Larry's whole day off by yelling at him, and she didn't know to apologize or modify her behavior because she didn't know she had done anything offensive. In counseling, Larry listed all of the times he was being yelled at, and Terry did not remember even one. Larry agreed to tell Terry each time he thought she was yelling at him so she would know.

This brings up another subject that Thinking and Feeling types often have to work out—when people are being critical and when they are being helpful.

Larry not only thought he was being yelled at: he also thought he was being criticized. Terry thought she was being helpful. Feeling types don't like criticism, and ironically, they are very critical of people who criticize them.

Thinking types will admit that they are critical, but most of the times they are charged with it they are merely being helpful.

Terry learned how to be helpful in a way that wouldn't hurt Larry's feelings. The next time he was making pancakes and using the metal spatula she could say something like, "I use the plastic one, or when I use the plastic one, the pan lasts longer."

Also, when a Feeling type presents an idea, it mustn't be greeted with "No, I have a different idea" because all sorts of trouble ensue.

Larry: I have an idea. Why don't we go to the zoo?
Terry: No. Let's go canoeing.

What Larry heard: You think my idea is stupid, and you won't even consider it. You think I'm stupid, too, and all you care about is your own ideas.
What Larry will do: He will go canoeing but will make sure that no one has a good time, even though today is a good day to canoe. He will reject each of Terry's ideas out of hand.

Larry: No, how 'bout if we see a baseball game?
Terry: I don't want to go all the way into the city. Why don't we see a movie?

What Larry heard: Terry is still interested in her own ideas and doesn't care about mine. I don't want to do anything.

What Terry heard: Larry is in a mood. It seems like no matter what I suggest, he turns it down without even giving me a reason.

> *Larry:* I just want to stay home.
> *Terry:* Great. That sounds like lots of fun.

Larry has crafted a lose-lose deal. His feelings are hurt, and he is getting even.

After counseling, they learned how to share ideas.

> *Larry:* Why don't we go to the zoo?
> *Terry:* That's a good idea. The zoo would be fun. My concern is that canoe rentals are half price this weekend, and it's going to be perfect weather. Why don't we go to the zoo when it's cloudy?
> *Larry:* You're right. Canoeing it is.

Step 3: Appreciate Types

Before people are aware of the Thinking/Feeling preference, they don't know the root of their concerns, so they can't articulate what's bothering them. Sometimes conflicts emerge because of the way that people react or their tone or their manner. People may analyze behavior like eye-rolling or sighing and take it to mean something greater than intended, and it may not be intended for anything. In therapy, people often say, "What did I say?" If you asked for a transcript, it would seem pretty innocuous, but not to the people involved.

Appreciation can go a long way:

> Dave and Maria are planning a family vacation for themselves and their three children. Dave is a Thinking type, and Maria is a Feeling type. They live in New Hampshire and want to visit Maria's parents in Michigan. All think this is a good idea.
>
> In past years they've flown. This year Dave thinks they should drive. But Maria thinks they should save in other areas

and fly. Maria is concerned that the car trip will be too long for the children. Dave said, "Sure they may be uncomfortable, but it's only a few days. They'll live.

Maria said, "Let's just buy the airplane tickets and find the money somehow." Dave said, "There is no money. I don't want to buy five tickets. We can't afford it."

They had reached an impasse.

Maria had to acknowledge to Dave that his money concerns were valid, and that she was thinking with her heart and hadn't taken the cost into consideration. Dave acknowledged that Maria was right in that a driving trip would be no fun for anyone.

Working together, they decided to buy Maria's parents tickets to see them in New Hampshire. Her parents thought that was a great idea, and in return, they rented a house on Lake Winnipesaukee for two weeks that was big enough for everyone.

Since Dave and Maria were able to take gut feelings one step further, they negotiated a solution that was good for all.

Until you and your spouse learn to express these gut feelings, you have to bring them out, and you bring out the underlying concerns by asking questions.

Step 4: Ask Open-Ended Questions

When you're trying to find underlying concerns that even your spouse doesn't know, ask open-ended questions. I teach this technique in Personality Selling®[1] classes for salespeople who want to understand customers' concerns. It's easy and works well. It's especially effective when the Introvert/Extrovert preference is kept in mind.

Open-ended questions can't be answered with one word. Open-ended questions need a more complete answer and should be used when you're gathering information. If you ask your spouse, "Is anything wrong?" you might get a closed-ended response of yes or no. Instead, by asking, "What should we do?" you will get a more complete answer.

When you ask, "What should we do?" you may at first hear "Nothing," or "It's impossible," or "There's nothing that can be done." Be relentless because if you gently prod and don't give up, you're bound to elicit the underlying concern.

Step 5: Use Closed-Ended Questions When You Want a Response

Closed-ended questions can be answered with only one word, usually yes or no. They are effective when you need very specific responses that leave no murky areas about what one is thinking. For instance, you may ask, "Do you want to go out to dinner tonight?" When you get a response, you'll know precisely that person's views on dinner, and you'll know if you need to go to the market. The beauty of a closed-ended question is that you'll get feedback of one sort or another.

Ask only one closed-ended question at a time, especially to Introverts who will process each question separately. Avoid a rapid-fire, "What do you think? How about if we order out Chinese? How about if we just stay home?" before you get an answer to any of the questions. The answer you get could be to your first, second, or third query, or to all three.

When you're explaining your concerns to a Thinking type, give a reason why you are concerned, and don't leave the person dangling with "It's just a feeling that I have."

With a Feeling type, comment on the person's emotional state as well as the situation that caused it.

One part of your goal is to understand someone's concerns. Another is to take hostility out of the equation.

Step 6: Detoxifying the Situation

Humans are emotional beings. We get angry from time to time. When there are pent-up emotions that haven't made it from gut level to actual words or feelings, anger is a signal that important concerns need addressing. Sometimes we know what these concerns are, but other times it takes some thought.

We may feel the tension building, but we ignore the evidence that anger is brewing. That happens when we're under stress and have a lot to do. We are overtired, the job is placing undue burdens on us, the bills are mounting up, the leaves need raking, the kids need braces, and April fifteenth is coming up fast—and we're not getting a refund.

With each stressor comes more pressure. We all know the feeling of forgetting trivial things (where are those keys?), getting easily perturbed at the slightest provocation, or being overwhelmed.

The brain is wired to give early warnings that life has gotten to be too much. Here are some others:

Many times marital conflict can be avoided if we pay attention to what our bodies are telling us. Your brain doesn't flash warning signs in your eyes like "slow down," but it does give some other indicators. Discovering and reacting to the indicators is called biofeedback. When the warning signal goes off, it's time to relax or slow life down. The yelling or hitting the wall or throwing items around that occurs at the end of the stress cycle can be nipped in the bud when we listen to our bodies.

If we have ignored the warnings, or if a serious event occurs and we get angry, that's part of being human. We're letting people know we have a concern. Remaining angry after people know there is a concern is counterproductive and can get in the way of addressing the concerns.

People may rant or repeat themselves or talk louder and louder because they feel that they're not being understood. But we tend to stop listening when others shout or restate a point. While all the haranguing is going on, the recipient's brain probably takes a break.

Your brain constantly monitors sounds. Your ears and brain have a partnership and can distinguish between background noise and actual conversations intended for you. (Your brain ignores background noise like a fan or an air conditioner, which is good or else those appliances would be incredibly distracting.) Why is this important to know in relationships?

When you are harangued, your brain categorizes the yelling as background noise. We've all been yelled at during our life. We know the feeling of tuning the yeller out and thinking about other things or most usually, negative "subvocalizations" about the person yelling. We think things like, "Will you shut up," or "What a jerk," or "Yap, yap, yap," or "Are you through yet?"

The point is that shouting or endless repetitions won't work. The goal of being listened to and understood can be accomplished in other ways.

If you have had a tendency to yell, realize that the goal of being listened to is backfiring. Try saying something like this: "I'm so frustrated because I feel like I'm not being understood or appreciated," or "I don't understand why my concern isn't treated as important."

If others yell at you, use the Stop! technique.[2] Put up your hand like a traffic cop and say "Stop!" It works wonders. (People often shout because they are insecure about their position. Pointing at them directly and saying "Stop!" is perceived as a threatening move that will only escalate the shouting.) Adding, "I really want to understand your concerns" further defuses the situation.

Addressing Types of Anger

We get angry with ourselves, with people outside the family, and with family members.

There's nothing wrong with getting angry. Anger is raw emotion, and it's part of being human. People who find themselves getting enraged a lot, however, (more than once a month?) need to consider if their criteria for getting angry is too fine. Let's consider each type of anger.

When we get angry with ourselves. Thinking types are more likely to be self-critical than Feeling types. Self-anger can eat us up inside.

Some people accept blame for events, even if they're not their fault; others don't accept blame for anything, even when it is their fault. Those who accept a lot of blame often do it to preserve harmony, but eventually, taking the rap for things they aren't responsible for takes its toll.

Getting angry with ourselves takes a lot of energy. Thinking types tend to berate themselves because they think they deserve it. Thinking types can be very harsh judges, and the sentences they pronounce on themselves tend to lack mercy.

Abe was supposed to mow the lawn on Saturday. It didn't really need it, but he planned to do it that day. That morning when he was running errands, he took the gas can along. As he was going by the gas station, an ambulance and two fire trucks went by. He pulled over to let all the emergency vehicles pass. He drove by the gas station as he was looking in his rearview mirror for more fire trucks.

When he got home he realized he forget to fill the gas can. He got really mad at himself, saying things like, "I can't believe I didn't fill the can," and "I'm so stupid."

To punish himself, he didn't go to the beach that afternoon as he was planning to do. He decided to get the gas during his favorite TV show in the afternoon as penance.

Abe needs to realize that people are always making mistakes, many each day. A good technique for Abe is imaging. Professional athletes use it to their advantage. Watch tennis players, basketball players, or golfers. Before they make a shot, they image in their minds how the shot should go. When they falter, they learn from their mistakes.

When Abe got home and realized that pulling over for the sirens caused him to forget the gas, he should have imaged. He should have told himself that when he's doing errands, he should consciously think about all of his tasks to complete if something happens to break his attention.

Feeling types tend to like harmony, and they don't understand Thinking types berating themselves. They'll say things like, "There's no need to get mad at yourself for such a stupid reason," or "Your temper tantrum is ruining our weekend."

The Feeling type's call to start harmonizing is about as effective as pouring gasoline on a fire. The Feeling type doesn't have the same appreciation for the gravity of missing an exit or forgetting to buy ice as the Thinking type does at that moment. The Thinking type, in time, will put the "tragic" events in perspective. While the Thinking type is expressing consternation, empathize; put it in perspective, but don't be condescending or patronizing.

Statement: I can't believe that I missed the exit. *(Hitting the steering wheel.)*

Response: I know it's frustrating to miss an exit and have to travel ten minutes south just to have to turn around and go back.

Statement: It is.

Response: You were right not to try to switch over three lanes. As much as we want to make time, you've been driving for three hours. We're not going to miss these twenty minutes, but if we got into an accident, it would have cost much more time and someone could have been seriously hurt.

Statement: You're right.

Response: (Later in the day.) When you missed the exit and you punched the steering wheel, I felt bad. It makes my trip pretty yucky when you get so mad at yourself. It's okay to get angry, but it would be better for me if you found a way that didn't involve yelling or punching the car.

Statement: You're right. I'm sorry.

When we get angry with people outside the family. We may become angry with coworkers or neighbors and want to lash out at them. But we restrain ourselves, externally giving no signs of conflict. Inside, however, we're seething.

Think of all that internal anger like pressure expanding in a balloon. Eventually, the balloon will pop. People will, too, but not always at the person they're angry with. When people become inappropriately enraged with others, almost certainly something happened earlier in the day or week that really ticked them off. They couldn't get upset at the time, so they yell at cars that cut them off on the highway or at their family members when they get home. Psychologists call this displacement.

Displacement can take three avenues; two of them are constructive. We know that hurting people is not constructive.

To be constructive, first realize you must let the pressure out of the balloon somehow. There are many ways to relieve stress: Silent prayer, meditation, or quiet works for some; exercise works for others. Whatever technique you use, the idea is to find a way to get rid of caustic energy.

The second way displacement can be dealt with is by intellectually reasoning that you're upset and that, under normal circumstances, your missing an exit, a baby's crying, a spouse's asking a favor, or a child's being late for dinner isn't a big deal and not something to get upset about.

Be honest. Tell your family members that you are very angry with your boss for making you work all weekend and they haven't done anything wrong. You're upset because of work. You will get the sympathy you need and deserve, and they won't wonder what they have done wrong or be edgy because of your moodiness.

When we get angry with family members. Getting angry with family members has serious and far-reaching effects. We'll have a relationship with these people for the rest of our lives. No matter how angry we get, productive responses are essential.

When anger bubbles, tell your spouse that you have concerns that need addressing, and arrange a time that will be good for both of you to collaborate. If anger resulted in unproductive behavior in the past, you can't change that. But you can learn from the past and make sure that the unproductive behavior is ancient history.

In this chapter we looked at what people get emotional about. Emotions add spice to life. They can be a signal that everything is okay or that there are concerns that need addressing. Remember that anger is a signal that there's a concern. Listen to the signal, and then turn it off.

Finally, Thinking and Feeling types are very different in their interpersonal relationships. Thinking types are often not trying to be mean or critical, nor are Feeling types trying to be so sensitive as to keep others walking on eggshells.

Next chapter we'll look at how people view time and how they make decisions.

What Happened
in the
Woods?

CHAPTER SIX

Two roads diverged in a wood, and I—
I took the one less traveled by,
And that has made all the difference.

Robert Frost,
"The Road Not Taken"

When the path in the wood diverges, some will be like Robert Frost and take the road less traveled. Sure, they'll say it has made all the difference because they'll find unexpected treasures or they'll have adventures few experience. But sometimes they'll get lost, hit dead ends without seeing anything of interest, or run out of gas in the middle of nowhere.

Others will take the road more traveled by, which is admittedly less poetic. This trip will be predictable. They'll get from point A to point B in the time they expected to. They'll miss interesting and surprising tidbits and adventures along the unexplored side trips. They'll say having a gloriously predictable trip has made all the difference; there's a reason that more people take the beaten path.

This chapter focuses in on the fourth personality area of Conflict Without Casualty, the Judging/Perceiving preference. This is the measure of our view on time and on decision making. Knowing how this operates can solve many strifes at home.

THE JUDGING/PERCEIVING PREFERENCE

If you're interested in discovering your type—which road you'll tend to take, answer the following questions.

Directions: Read each statement and check A or B next to the response, depending on which fits you better. There aren't any right, wrong, or better answers. You'll find information on scoring the test at the end.

1. **I tend to like days that are:**
   ☐ A) spontaneous.
   ☐ B) tightly scheduled.

2. **When I make a significant decision, I usually:**
   ☐ A) take as much time as I need.
   ☐ B) allot myself time to make it.

3. **When I am going someplace, it's more fun to:**
   ☐ A) play it by ear.
   ☐ B) plan the route in advance.

4. **When I make a bad decision, I feel:**
   ☐ A) like I was rushed.
   ☐ B) I did the best I could, given the time constraints.

5. **If I'm given a deadline for doing something and there's not enough time, I:**
   ☐ A) allow the deadline to slip until I have all the data.
   ☐ B) make it anyway, with the data I've got.

6. **After choosing one of many options, I am most likely to be:**
   ☐ A) relieved.
   ☐ B) concerned.

7. **If I overloaded my appointment calendar one day, I would:**
   ☐ A) try to reschedule some appointments.
   ☐ B) try to keep all the appointments, even if it was difficult.

8. **I think it's important to have a:**
- [ ] A) general sense of time.
- [ ] B) concrete sense of time.

9. **I'm usually:**
- [ ] A) late.
- [ ] B) early.

10. **When I make a major purchase:**
- [ ] A) I decide when I am comfortable that I have enough information.
- [ ] B) I set up a time frame for making a final decision, and then work to get all the information by that deadline.

11. **After using something, I generally put it away:**
- [ ] A) in the most convenient place.
- [ ] B) where I'd be most likely to look for it next time I use it.

TOTALS

_____ A

_____ B

Scoring: Add the number of responses scored in the A column and the B column, and put your totals at the bottom. If you scored six or more "A" responses, your preference is more likely a Perceiving type. If you scored six or more "B" responses, you're more likely a Judging type.

Here's a list of words and phrases that typify how Judging and Perceiving types think and look at the world.

Words and Phrases Typical of Judging
and Perceiving Types

Judging	*Perceiving*
What's the deadline?	What event needs to happen?
Lost time	Make time

Words and Phrases Typical of Judging
and Perceiving Types—*Cont'd*

Judging	*Perceiving*
Focus	Chill
We're running late	We have lots to do
Schedule	Flexible
Everything in its place	I'm better under pressure
It's time	Are we ready?

Judging and Perceiving types view time differently. Judging types have a concrete sense of time and like making plans and schedules and adhering to them. When faced with a decision, they seek closure. Perceiving types have a general concept of time and like minimal schedules; they dislike deadlines and want to keep their options open. Judging types tend to write appointments in calendars or keep them in the forefront of their minds. Perceiving types tend to stick Post-it Notes on the refrigerator or take life one hour at a time.

Let's say that someone wants to buy a new car and needs transportation quickly. A Judging type in this pickle sets a time he thinks is reasonable for looking for a car, perhaps a week. He'll look at as many cars as he can in the week and buy the one he likes best at the end of the deadline. (His Introvert/Extrovert, Sensing/Intuitive, and Thinking/Feeling preferences will determine the manner in which he looks.) If a Judging type finds a better car the week after, he won't ruminate over it because he'll reason that he made the best decision he could given the time constraints.

A Perceiving type has certain concerns that need to be dealt with before she is comfortable deciding. She might be concerned that the car has good gas mileage, an air bag, and payments of less than two hundred dollars a month. She'll decide in a day if she finds a car that meets her requirements in a day, or she'll decide in a month if it takes that long.

Perceiving types are often reproached for being indecisive. Actually, they're not indecisive. Perceiving types are careful decision makers. Though they may take an extra week to buy a car, they'll be very happy with it for the several years that they'll own it. If they needed a car for work and they were forced to make a decision before all their criteria were met, the entire time they had the car, they would have a lingering feeling they could have done better.

GENERAL CONFLICT WITHOUT CASUALTY TECHNIQUES WITH JUDGING AND PERCEIVING TYPES

We already know that Perceiving types will take the road less traveled by and Judging types the one more traveled by. But what's going on during the journey?

Step 1: Consider Schedules and Timing

When you deal with Judging types, set up a schedule with them. They'll usually keep to it. When you work with Perceiving types, find out what they need to know, what problems need solutions, and the sequence of events that need to take place before they'll act. If they're reluctant to commit on a direction to take, reinforce the benefits or necessity of finally deciding.

The experience of time is very different to Judging and Perceiving types. Viewing the passage of time differently can create all sorts of confusion, problems, animosity, and stress, most of which can be avoided by understanding the types.

When Judging types are faced with a situation, they immediately set up an internal time schedule for what needs to be done, how long the task and subtasks are going to take, and when things need to be wrapped up. Ask Judging types if they are hungry, and they'll look at their watch and calculate how long it was since the last meal before telling you. Ask Judging types if they are over- or underweight, and they'll get on a scale and compare the weight on the scale to a weight chart.

Perceiving types set up an internal *event* schedule that includes all the milestones that need to be achieved but with an approximate time frame for when they will happen. Ask Perceiving types if they are hungry, and they'll analyze their hunger pains. They won't look at a watch because they probably won't have one. (Perceiving types with a watch usually confess that it was a present and they use it as a fashion accessory.) Perceiving types look at themselves in a mirror to decide whether they are happy with their weight, though they'll use a Judging type's scale, too, if it's available.

Step 2: Understand Advantages and Disadvantages of Being a Judging Type

Judging types will keep to schedules and meet deadlines. When Judging types say they will be somewhere at 10:00 A.M. on Saturday, they will be. Knowing this tendency can make planning and scheduling easy.

> Liz is a Judging type. She knows that to get to work on time, she needs to wake up her son at 7:30 because it will take fifteen minutes to get him ready, ten minutes to get to day care, four to five minutes to schmooze with the baby-sitter, and forty-five minutes to drive to work. (She also knows that if it rains, traffic will be slower, so the drive to work takes seven minutes longer.)
>
> Before Liz embarks on any trip or starts any project, she analyzes all of the aspects of the task and does a brief time analysis for each part. She almost always arrives on time and finishes tasks in time.

Judging types excel at having a concrete sense of the length of jobs and the level of effort required to complete them. They keep an eye on the finish line and won't be easily distracted.

The flip side to being a Judging type is that people will sometimes create for themselves self-imposed deadlines that they believe *have* to be met but, in reality, can't or shouldn't be. Then they may be overly hasty in decision making.

> Liz had a particularly busy day at work ahead of her. When Billy, her son, was slow getting ready, she hurried him along. Still, she fell nine to ten minutes behind schedule. So, instead of spending their normal seven minutes together having breakfast, she gave him a Pop-Tart in the car.
>
> When they got to the baby-sitter's, she realized that she forgot to bring Billy's earache medicine. The few minutes that

she saved by rushing to keep on schedule cost her twenty-five since she had to go home and get the medicine.

What Liz did that day is very common for a Judging type—creating self-imposed deadlines. She set a time limit, independent of when a task must be completed.

Judging types like closure, or the sense that something is completed or on its way to being finished. That keeps Judging types on schedule. However, having unrealistic deadlines creates unnecessary stress for all involved.

Realities such as construction and accidents that cause delays will frustrate Judging types to no end because their schedules are being messed with. They are needlessly frustrated because they have no control over the situation. Judging types need to constantly remind themselves that getting anxious won't move traffic any better and, in fact, exacerbates the situation.

Before taking a vacation on Friday, Liz wanted Billy and her husband, Bill, to be ready by Tuesday. That way, everything would be "all set."

It was very difficult for Bill to be packed by Tuesday with all the loose ends he had to tie at work. To him, this "hurry up and stop" mentality didn't make going on vacation very fun.

Other times deadlines get in the way of unexpected fun for Judging types:

Bruno planned his yearly cellar cleaning on the first Saturday in May. The night before, his neighbor called him and offered him four box seat tickets at Fenway Park that couldn't be used because of a family emergency.

Bruno turned the tickets down, even though he and his family loved watching the Red Sox and had never had seats behind the dugout. To him, the plan of cleaning the cellar—which could be done anytime—could not be altered.

That Saturday, he and his family weren't happy sweeping the cellar instead of being at the game, and they wished that he could have been offered the tickets any other Saturday.

Schedules of all sorts are important to Judging types, not only keeping to them, but also thinking about them and making them. They always know when bills need to be paid. They never miss the start of a movie or a TV program because they check the TV schedule at the beginning of the week.

If you're a Judging type, as you formulate your internal time schedule, constantly ask yourself, is this a real deadline or an artificial one? Are the schedules necessary?

If you're married to a Judging type, give your spouse tasks involving planning or time sensitivity. If you feel that a Judging type's deadlines are self-imposed, ask whether the deadline is real or important only to him or her. You may want to paint a worst-case scenario.

The next year when they were offered tickets on cellar cleaning day (what are the odds?), Bruno's wife asked him what would happen if they cleaned the basement some other time. He told her that he always cleaned the cellar the first Saturday in May and he has been doing so since he was twelve. If he didn't do it then, it would never get done.

She persisted, "What would be the worst case? Why can't we do it next weekend? How many chances will we get to take the kids to box seats at Fenway? I asked the dust and the sleds and the snow shovels, and they don't mind hanging out for a few days."

Bruno said, "You're right. Let's go."

Many times Judging types realize that their self-imposed deadlines are keeping them from participating in fun events. They're usually very happy when people give them permission to change the schedule (which is why so many of them marry Perceiving types). Bruno had a great time at the game, and his cellar got cleaned the next weekend. Everyone won.

Now, let's look at the Perceiving type.

Step 3: Understand Advantages and Disadvantages of Being a Perceiving Type

Perceiving types live less structured lives than Judging types. They're very inventive and flexible. Changes in plans will not fluster them. Still, they're reluctant to come to closure until certain events have transpired, which can make seemingly simple decisions laborious. (Sometimes Perceiving types carefully think out small decisions and discover that they weren't so simple at all.) They're also creative and industrious problem solvers because they are used to doing things in a nonstandard way.

> Paula is a Perceiving type. Her husband, Jimmy, is a Judging type. He was making cookies for her at Christmastime and realized that the recipe called for using a flour sifter. Since he didn't have one, he was about to throw away the wet ingredients and make brownies. Paula said, "Stop. Let me fix this." To Jimmy's amazement, Paula began sifting the flour with a cheese grater—and it worked!

The Perceiving types' ability to rescue recipes gone awry, their laid-back attitude, and their feeling that there's nothing you can do today that you can't do tomorrow make them fun to be around.

The United States is a country that favors Judging types. Structure is expected, and promptness is regarded not only as a virtue but also as a necessity. Italy is a country that favors Perceiving types. Everything is late, and no one cares.

Perceiving types get frustrated at all the deadlines they're expected to meet. Companies like Federal Express love Perceiving types because they put off paying the mortgage until the last day possible, and they fork over the money needed to overnight it. In fact, Perceiving types are so used to paying late fees and missing early bird specials that they don't even blink twice when it happens. To them, it's just a cost of living among Judging types.

Frustration can set in when a Judging type tries to rush them or pressure them into a decision that they're not ready to make. Perceiving types decide on an event schedule, but most don't know that. All they know is that they have an uneasy feeling or aren't yet ready.

If you're a Perceiving type, realize the strength in your decision-making process and be glad for it. Even though you make fewer decisions than others, you almost always are careful in making them.

If you're a Judging type, ask Perceiving types what needs to happen before they'll feel comfortable. Then work to make those events occur.

THE FOUR TEMPERAMENTS

Anytime people share one or two preferences, there will be some similarities in the way they deal with others or want to be dealt with. Still, there are four combinations of two preferences in which the similarities are so striking, they're categorized separately. Psychologists call them temperaments. (Remember that Jungian-type shorthand uses the first letter of a preference, except that Intuitive is N because the I is taken up with Introvert.) The four temperaments are: (1) Intuitive/Feeling (NF), (2) Intuitive/Thinking (NT), (3) Sensing/Judging (SJ), and (4) Sensing/ Perceiving (SP).

1. Intuitive/Feeling (NF)

These people like possibilities and the search for meaning. They spend their lives trying to understand behavior and people. Since there are an unlimited number of emotions and possibilities to consider, their quest is often unfinished. NFs tend to be sensitive to the needs of others, but they can spend so much time attending to others' needs that they neglect themselves. NFs are generally not materialistic; they seek relationships over possessions.

NFs tend to like and understand poetry, symbolism, and allegorical thinking. They have great imaginations and can picture things in their minds easily. They make others feel special and want to feel special themselves.

When certain behaviors upset them, they analyze the situation in their heads. Since they have to gauge all possible meanings of all possible emotions, this process can take a while. If they are hurt by criticism, disharmony, or cruelty, their tendency is to think of the meanest thing they can possibly say, and then say it. The problem is that what triggered all the emotional turmoil could have taken place ten minutes, ten hours, or ten days beforehand. It's understandable that the recipient(s) of the barb may be confused.

NFs find life easier when they discern personal criticism from impersonal statements and bring up concerns sooner rather than later so that they can be addressed. The apostle John, "the one Jesus loved," was an NF.

2. *Intuitive/Thinking (NT)*

When faced with a dilemma, NTs look at every alternative and carefully and systematically rate each option with the best solution percolating to the top. At a very early age NTs try to improve their environment. They do this by experimenting and dissecting appliances. Of course, this tendency can be disconcerting to parents of NT children who wonder what would happen if they put butter in the dog's ears. Parents of NT children need to nip the electrical, chemical, and radioactive material experiments in the bud ASAP or else risk losing both house and NT.

NTs constantly try to find the best way of doing things. They value competence in themselves and their ideas, and they will be insulted if people belittle the fruit of their thought.

In their zeal to analyze all possibilities, NTs are likely to expend great effort on unworkable or unfeasible options. They tend to go down many wrong paths. On the other hand, not being restricted by practicality yields interesting and unexpected results.

When dealing with NTs, instead of focusing on what's wrong, give them another possibility to consider. They can analyze and rate it along with their other thoughts. The apostle Peter was an NT.

3. *Sensing/Judging (SJ)*

SJs combine the practicality of their Sensing side with the planning of their Judging side. SJs tend to hold traditional values and to delay gratification. Thus, they tend to be good at saving money.

Their Sensing side makes them detail oriented. They are good at seeing faults in a plan before it happens, and they usually want to wait to begin a project until every contingency is taken care of. That is why SJs and NTs get into so many arguments. NTs try to simplify the complicated, look at tasks as manageable, and hope to problem solve on the fly. In their commitment to be careful, SJs sometimes complicate a simple problem far beyond its merit. While NTs are off and running, SJs are begging for restraint.

For example, SJs tend to be members of churches that are conservative and hold traditional values and preach restraint. The apostle Paul was an SJ.

4. Sensing/Perceiving (SP)

SPs like to live on the edge. SPs enjoy events (such as skiing and racing) and occupations (such as police work and fire fighting) that involve physical activity, and they often like the thrill of danger.

SP's tend to disdain rules and regulations and societal standards. That disdain leads the charge in times of oppression. Thomas Jefferson, Carrie Nation, Rosa Parks, Mahatma Gandhi, Martin Luther King, Jr., the students at Tienanmen Square, Anwar Sadat, and Alexander Solzhenitsyn are some of the many SPs throughout history who have challenged rules for their injustice, even though doing so was dangerous for them.

WHAT IS JESUS' TYPE?

A lot of people wonder about Jesus' type. Theologians who are also familiar with Jungian psychology, on which type is based, took the Myers-Briggs Type Indicator (MBTI) and answered the questions as they would expect Jesus to. They concluded that, as one might expect, Jesus is a special case. He combines the best of all the types and has all of the characteristics of each type.

The last four chapters looked at the four dimensions of personality. The Introvert/Extrovert preference determines how we think and how much human interaction we find most comfortable. The Sensing/Intuitive preference determines if we like the details or the big picture, and how information to convince us or others is best presented. The Thinking/Feeling preference is useful for revealing how we develop concerns and emotions. Finally, the Judging/Perceiving preference determines how we make decisions and our view on time.

Next, we'll look at how we put all the preferences together, because the preferences in combination reveal more about us than any of them can individually.

In the last section of the book, we'll look at how to merge and use personality type and conflict resolution style in relationships.

Character Traits
of the
Personality Types

CHAPTER SEVEN

Y ou may have already figured out that with four areas of Conflict Without Casualty, each with a choice of two preferences, there is a total of sixteen personality types.

WHAT IS YOUR DOMINANT FUNCTION?

Part of Conflict Without Casualty is recognizing the importance of your dominant, or favorite, function. Also, be aware that any activity involving your inferior, or least favorite, function can be frustrating or annoying for you. You also need to recognize your spouse's dominant and inferior functions.

Psychologists say that everyone has a dominant function and an inferior function. The dominant function is the preference in the middle two letters, S/N or T/F, that's the best developed—the one a person relies on most.

If you are an Extroverted Judging type, your third letter (either T or F) is your dominant function. If you're Extroverted Perceiving, the second letter (S or N) is dominant.

An Introverted Judging type has a dominant second letter (either S or N); for Introverted Perceiving Types, their third letter (T or F) is dominant.

The second function is the person's "other" middle letter. The inferior function is the weakest and least developed. It's not part of the personality type. A person with a dominant Thinking function has an inferior Feeling function.

When solving problems, focus your efforts on the dominant

and secondary functions and away from the inferior function. For instance, an ENTJ (Extroverted, Intuitive, Thinking, Judging type) has a dominant Thinking function and an inferior Feeling function. Sell an ENTJ on the impersonal logic of the solution (the dominant Thinking function), and not the happiness and harmony the solution will generate (the inferior Feeling function).

I/E	*J/P*	*Dominant*
E	J	Third (T or F)
E	P	Second (S or N)
I	J	Second (S or N)
I	P	Third (T or F)

THE IMPORTANCE OF THE DOMINANT FUNCTION

Focus on the dominant function to get to the heart of people's concerns. For example, someone with a dominant Sensing function won't commit until she has all the facts and is sure that the solution is practical.

When you discover your dominant function and the dominant functions of your spouse and everyone with whom you deal, understanding will increase, and agreement will come more readily.

How Perceiving Types Decide

Solving problems to the dominant function is especially necessary when you're dealing with Perceiving types because they are careful decision makers who won't be bound by time deadlines. If the issue of the negotiation directly relates to the dominant function of a Perceiving type, address that function during the negotiation. If Perceiving types are considering something outside their dominant function, they'll value it as less important and usually make the decision easily.

For instance, suppose a Perceiving type with a dominant Feeling function (INFP or ISFP) is buying office supplies. He will decide quickly which wastebasket to buy because the color, style, and size won't do anything to affect office harmony or job satisfaction. That decision will be easy. But if that same Perceiving type is buying a puppy for the family, he will agonize over the decision because he knows a puppy can be a joy, a bother, or a disaster to a home environment. This customer with a dominant Feeling function will worry about getting the right size dog with the right temperament. And the question of whether getting a puppy is a good idea will weigh on him.

THE IMPORTANCE OF THE INFERIOR FUNCTION

The inferior function is the preference opposite of your dominant function. For example, dominant Feeling types have an inferior function of Thinking, and vice versa.

The inferior function comes out when we are under a great deal of stress. Stress is really a bad time for this function to come out because it's our most undeveloped and ineffective function. Their inferior Feeling function will hit dominant Thinking types at the worst times. Some people may think, *So what's the problem? They just become a little nicer and more considerate.* Wrong.

When the inferior Feeling function emerges, people don't become concerned with meaning and harmony; they become randomly emotional. In fact, in an extreme situation some people think they are going insane, which they are not. As soon as the stressor is relieved, they're back to normal.

Here's what happens during inferior function episodes. Dominant Sensing types who like looking at facts and practicalities will start analyzing wild possibilities. This can be very frightening for the folks who value their practicality. They, too, can think there is something wrong with them.

Dominant Intuitive types will stop considering possibilities and will become excessively rigid. Their inferior Sensing episodes will be marked by a gloom-and-doom mood that nothing will work and that all is lost, which it isn't.

Dominant Feeling types will, for brief periods, be as mean as they possibly can. They'll think of the worst thing they can say and say it. Sometimes they'll berate themselves for being so ruthless, but they'll be back to their old-feeling selves soon enough.

The Remedy for the Inferior Function

The remedy for the emergence of the inferior function is to realize that it's stress driven. If you or someone you know is acting atypically, realize that the behavior is tied to anxiety. You need to reduce or remove the stress. Consult a physician for the best way for you, but methods include taking a deep breath, learning relaxation techniques, getting a massage, reducing the workload, delegating tasks, and sometimes taking prescription medication.

If your anxiety is acute, take a deep breath and tell your partner that you want to work out the situation, but you need some time to collect your thoughts and your energies.

UNDERSTANDING THE SIXTEEN PERSONALITY TYPES

Putting all the letters together adds to a knowledge of how personality type explains aspects of our behavior and how we interact with others.

Below, you'll find brief descriptions of each type along with behavioral clues associated with each preference.

1. *ESTJ*

Dominant:	Thinking
Secondary:	Sensing
Inferior:	Feeling

ESTJs like traditional values, with family and marriage being two of the stalwarts that they will protect. They want everyone to be taken care of on a long-term basis. ESTJs are likely to advocate short-term pain if they perceive benefits in the future.

ESTJs, like all SJs, consider discipline within the family to be a positive element, especially for children. They will tend to focus on little infractions and frequently discuss why they are meting out discipline.

What they look for in a mate. Since the inferior function is Feeling, they tend to look for Feeling types to provide and teach them to express warmth and caring. Also, with the STJ combination causing them to live a structured life, they tend to look for a spouse who is a Perceiving type.

They may seek a spouse who is a Sensing type because ESTJs tend to think of Intuitives as having their heads in the clouds. On the other hand, they may find an Intuitive's "wild" ideas refreshing.

2. *ESTP*
Dominant:	Sensing
Secondary:	Thinking
Inferior:	Intuitive

ESTPs like living for the moment. They like participating in sports and making or fixing things with their hands. They like to rally the forces and inspire people. They aren't worriers, which is a double-edged sword. They won't waste energy on anxious worry that's uncalled for. They always assume that everything will work out, so life's events don't throw them, even those that need attention.

What they look for in a mate. They look for a spouse who is a worrier—someone who will watch out for the rent and important bills—so they'll often pick a Judging mate.

3. *ESFJ*
Dominant:	Feeling
Secondary:	Sensing
Inferior:	Thinking

ESFJs are warm, talkative, gregarious, cooperative, and easy to be around. They like harmony and will avoid situations that are potentially not harmonious. They like being with people and will avoid solitude like the plague.

What they look for in a mate. They want a spouse who is fun. ESFJs tend to marry Introverts who are looking for action. They also will marry any type that values harmony, which is why they'll usually avoid dominant Thinking types. Because they seek fun, they're attracted to SPs who live for the moment.

4. *ESFP*
Dominant:	Sensing
Secondary:	Feeling
Inferior:	Intuitive

ESFPs love being with other people. They are adept noticers of details about people's mannerisms and voice tones, and they often pelt friends with marshmallows by poking fun at their individual characteristics. They're very good impressionists and storytellers.

All these traits make them warm, witty, and outstanding conversationalists. Also, their combination of realism and concern for others makes them excellent crisis solvers. They often take on the role of mediator.

What they look for in a mate. ESFPs like harmony and want Thinking types to bounce ideas off, but not ones that are confrontational. Because they are spontaneous, they look for Judging types to add the planning dimension so that their ideas can be carried through and flourish.

5. ENFP

Dominant:	Intuitive
Secondary:	Feeling
Inferior:	Sensing

ENFPs constantly search for the next thing to explore. They're often students of life and like to talk about and develop theories of human behavior. They are very social, and if they are home alone, they will make a beeline for the phone and talk to friends.

What they look for in a mate. ENFPs often hook up with ISTJs, their opposite type. As they are pursuing and discovering life's significance, they need someone to balance the checkbook and be a stabilizing force. They intellectually know they need this, but the same stability that the ISTJ offers can often be the source of conflict.

6. ENFJ

Dominant:	Feeling
Secondary:	Intuitive
Inferior:	Thinking

ENFJs' strength is the greatness they see in others. They muster the talents of others and figure out ways to bring them to the fullest. Like ENFPs, they like exploring and being adventuresome. They'll lead by example. They spend a typical day off thinking of fun things for the family to do and then planning to make it happen. Their dominant Feeling function will gently encourage people to keep to the schedule.

What they look for in a mate. ENFJs, like all dominant Feeling types, want harmony. They'll seek someone who shares their quest for knowledge and exploration. They may become frustrated if someone is content and doesn't want to expand the mind or seek a variety of experiences.

7. *ENTP*

Dominant:	Intuitive
Secondary:	Thinking
Inferior:	Sensing

ENTPs are good with language and are constantly joking. They like debating issues and sometimes find arguing a sport. When faced with a problem, they'll begin talking about possible solutions as they logically analyze each one. This can be disconcerting to Introverts who want to mull over a problem silently. Because they don't have a strongly developed sense of closure, they can continue a conversation for a long time.

What they look for in a mate. ENTPs want a spouse who will appreciate their inventiveness and humor.

8. *ENTJ*

Dominant:	Thinking
Secondary:	Intuitive
Inferior:	Feeling

ENTJs are very good at problem solving and leading. They enjoy taking over and adding structure and fairness at work and in families. When they make a decision, they are certain that it will work out, and it usually will. Their secondary Intuitive function sometimes misses important details so mistakes can be big ones.

ENTJs value competence in themselves and others.

What they look for in a mate. ENTJs want to accomplish as much as they can, so they'll look for a mate who allows them to. Since ENTJs can be harsh with people they consider incompetent or people who have done an injustice to them or to others, ENTJs want a mate that will be warm and caring.

9. ISTJ

Dominant:	Sensing
Secondary:	Thinking
Inferior:	Intuitive

ISTJs are definitely people you would leave your million dollars in cash with when you go away for a week. Of all the types, they are the most practical, orderly, and cautious. Their word is their bond. Your money would be safe and would probably grow in value.

What they look for in a mate. They want to share their carefulness with people who would benefit from it. They also are looking for people who know how to plan fun things to do. Since they tend to be serious, they like mates who encourage them to lighten up.

10. ISTP

Dominant:	Thinking
Secondary:	Sensing
Inferior:	Feeling

ISTPs quietly analyze all that's going on around them and debate it internally. They want to know how and why things work and what can be improved. World-class athletes are often ISTPs because they frequently train alone, they have to be precise, and they continue training until they reach some event, like an award or physical feat.

What they look for in a mate. ISTPs have a large cache of interesting insights locked inside their heads. They want to share their thoughts with a partner who will elicit them. Also, they want a spouse to appreciate that there are times they want to spend alone.

11. ISFJ

Dominant:	Sensing
Secondary:	Feeling
Inferior:	Intuitive

ISFJs are great observers of other people. They tend to be very social, though they will have only a few very good friends. They often find interesting quirks of personality and habits and poke fun at others by imitating them. If you have been imitated, you know you are in good company with the ISFJ.

What they look for in a mate. They look for a mate who likes a lot of sociability and is a good conversationalist. They also want a spouse who is not critical of them and appreciates them for who they are.

12. ISFP

Dominant:	Feeling
Secondary:	Sensing
Inferior:	Thinking

ISFPs are quite soft-spoken, good-natured, and creative. As it is to INFPs, life is a serious matter. Often they can notice nuances of behavior and can appropriately or inappropriately tie meaning to them. They like being part of a group but don't like being the leader. They are relaxed about deadlines and take life one day at a time.

What they look for in a mate. They look for someone to act as a stabilizing force that helps them achieve goals with understanding. Also, a helping nature motivates them to seek a spouse and family that they can aid.

13. INFP

Dominant:	Feeling
Secondary:	Intuitive
Inferior:	Thinking

Harmony is the watchword for INFPs. Their nature also dictates that they observe and contemplate all that goes on around them (I), think of what it means (N) and its effect on important people in their lives (F). This introspection is ongoing (P).

This leads to a flurry of activity inside the INFP brain. INFPs hate rejection, especially of dreams and theories close to the heart. They'll benefit from learning to share their ideas without prompting.

What they look for in a mate. INFPs have lots going on internally and are easy and fun to be around. They seek mates who will provide a steadying force and will encourage them to pursue ideas, beliefs, and interests.

14. INFJ

Dominant:	Intuitive
Secondary:	Feeling
Inferior:	Sensing

INFJs are quiet innovators. They are like their counterparts, INFPs, in that they are constantly contemplating thoughts and are very deep emotionally. INFJs take significant dates very seriously. Because of this, holidays, birthdays, and anniversaries assume special meaning of their own.

What they look for in a mate. INFJs look for a mate who will appreciate their insights and allow them lots of Introverted time. Because they spend so much time attaching meaning to events, they like spouses who are thick-skinned so they don't have to walk on eggshells on a regular basis.

15. INTP

Dominant:	Thinking
Secondary:	Intuitive
Inferior:	Feeling

INTPs are good problem solvers, yet their Introverted Perceiving nature causes them to have lingering doubts about their solutions; they ponder their actions for a long time after making a decision.

The upside is, their Introverted Perceiving nature keeps them from coming to premature closure, so their decisions are good ones.

What they look for in a mate. INTPs look for mates who will support their decisions and help minimize their worrying and regret.

16. INTJ

Dominant:	Intuitive
Secondary:	Thinking
Inferior:	Sensing

INTJs are good at problem solving and designing plans or houses. They take a no-nonsense approach to planning family vacations by considering the goals of each member of the family and internally debating each alternative. Still, they tend to be creative and decisive.

What they look for in a mate. They look for someone who is talkative and can appreciate their creativity and problem solving. They spend time alone constantly developing plans and theories, but they want to share them with someone.

In this chapter we've looked at the dominant and inferior functions. When we make important decisions, our dominant function needs to be appeased; and if we're under stress, our inferior function takes over our personality. Also, the four preferences together yield lots of information about who we are and what we like.

Chapter 2 looked at conflict resolution which is behavioral. Chapters 3 through 7 looked at several personality traits. In the next chapter we'll go over patterns, another learned aspect of how we act.

Relationship Patterns

CHAPTER EIGHT

This chapter explains patterns. Patterns in general psychological terms are ways of behaving or situations we tend to live out many times over.

One member of a couple may view predictability as comforting and enjoy the pattern; the other may look at the same situation and see it as being in a rut. Many times when one or both members of a couple are unhappy, it's because, unbeknownst to them, their lives have entered into patterns.

HEALTHY AND DESTRUCTIVE PATTERNS

Couples enter into healthy, meaningless, and destructive patterns. Understanding these patterns promotes the well-being of a relationship. The idea is, of course, that if you recognize a destructive pattern, you change it. If you are struggling in this area, friends and therapists can help see patterns that to you are concealed.

Relationship patterns take several forms. Conflict resolution style is a pattern that we talked about in chapter 2. But others are called scripts and games. We'll look at scripts first. A script is a predictable pattern where everyone knows and plays a part. Cues, in theater lingo, are the actors' and actresses' signals to do something. Couples act out scripts on cue too.

SCRIPTS

Everyone has heard of Pavlov, the psychologist who rang a bell whenever he fed his dogs. He discovered that dogs got all excited and drooled when they knew it was suppertime. The dogs associated hearing the bell with dinner. When Pavlov rang the bell but didn't have any Alpo waiting, the dogs still got excited and drooled. They associated the stimulus (the bell) with the response (the food). The technical term for this is *classical conditioning*.

Even though we're a lot more complex than dogs are, certain stimuli, both positive and negative, get us going. Usually, we don't realize that we've been conditioned, but we have. Let's look at how a couple I'll call Fredda and James conditioned each other.

Both Fredda and James are twenty-four years old, and they have been married two years. Fredda has a Trans Am, and she has had it since she was in college. When James washes and waxes her car, she is very appreciative. Having a sparkling car to ride in makes her feel sexy and brings back fond memories of college. She likes to drive around the campus, and she enjoys the college men looking at her driving her shiny sports car. She always thinks, *Too bad. You can't have me because I'm married to an awesome guy who even washes my car.* James gives the car a makeover about once a month.

James told me one of the things he likes about his sexual relationship with Fredda is when she initiates lovemaking. I asked him how often he thought that was, and he told me every few weeks. Neither James nor Fredda made the connection, but the only time it happened was after he waxed the Trans Am.

Both James and Fredda thought Fredda taking the initiative was an enjoyable part of lovemaking. When they no longer behaved like Pavlov's dogs, their sex life was more interesting.

Other times patterns can be ugly.

Rita and Ken have been married for five years and have two children. Ken frequently laments Rita's lack of sexual desire since their second child arrived. He is also not happy that she is fifteen pounds more than her prepregnancy weight.

When Ken is feeling particularly down, he calls Rita frigid, which disturbs her greatly. To make him feel that her sexual interest has not diminished, she performs oral sex, though she doesn't particularly enjoy it. Then she has sex with him while they are both standing, which he enjoys, but she finds it uncomfortable and impossible to have an orgasm.

For several days afterward, he compliments her on her looks, which she likes.

The pattern works like this:

1. Ken is mean.
2. Rita feels bad about herself.
3. Ken continues to be mean.
4. Rita performs sexually to please Ken.
5. Ken is nice to Rita for a few days.

After several months of this pattern—a pattern that neither knew existed until it was pointed out to them—Rita became more withdrawn. Sexual intimacy became unpleasant for her.

Ken realized subconsciously that in order to be sexually gratified in the way that was best for him, he would have to (1) be verbally abusive to Rita and (2) be sexually active in ways that Rita did not like. Ken learned in marriage counseling that Rita did not like performing oral sex or making love standing. Ken would have no way of knowing that. Rita performed the acts to reinforce her sexiness to Ken, so while, to her, she was going through the motions, she seemed, to him, to delight in them.

At the beginning of counseling, I asked Ken what Rita liked sexually. He told me that she liked oral sex and sexual intercourse in bed and against the wall.

Rita blurted out, "How can you say I like those things? Can't you tell that I'm not enjoying myself?"

I asked Rita how Ken would know that. She told me, "He can tell by the way I look, the way I sound. He knew I didn't like it, but all he cared about was meeting his needs."

I explained to them about the Read My Mind Game (see pages 127–28), and then I asked Ken if he had any idea she was sending him negative signals. He said no.

Then I asked him why he was making these insulting jabs: "You're frigid," "Your body isn't what it used to be," and "It's too bad you can't wear your old clothes."

Ken said that Rita once told him that she used to like it when they had more time for each other sexually before their children were born. When she saw pictures of herself before she had kids, she would say things like, "I wish I could look like that again." He said, "I was trying to encourage her. I figured that if I was a little mean to her, she'd get sick of me bothering her and do something about it."

Feeling attractive was important to Rita. Ken's insults *did* motivate her to perform sexually, but not without a cost. There was a stimulus-response pattern. The stimulus was an insult, and the response was to prove the insult wrong by acting sexy in Ken's eyes.

Stimulus-response, as in this case, works aversively. In time Rita started hating Ken for ringing the bell, and hating herself for responding to him. Then Ken himself, not just the verbal jabs, became the stimulus that made Rita anxious, and hateful feelings were activated when he walked in the room.

Ken didn't realize that subconsciously, she would submit to his favorite sexual practices every time he insulted her.

One note before continuing. The practice of insulting or hurting someone or constantly having the threat of harm on one's mind in order to motivate behavior is destructive. This is called *operant conditioning,* a term coined by B. F. Skinner. He said that using negative reinforcement with people should *never* be done. (We know that it's effective because in Nazi concentration camps guards would attain ultimate control, but the people felt less than human and demoralized.)

When some people are put down, their tendency is to counter-attack and parry with a barb of their own or to say, "Buzz off!" Others internalize the criticism and, like Rita, adapt their behavior to prove the insulter wrong, yet feel a sea of torrent in their hearts. Eventually, like Rita, people say enough is enough. They can't stand it anymore, and the ensuing resentment will diminish or even devastate the relationship.

Breaking the Pattern

People who find themselves in predicaments like Rita's can stop the cycle by breaking the pattern. The situation would have been halted early on if Rita had said, "You know, Ken, calling me frigid or unattractive doesn't make me feel sexy. Not only does it not turn me on, but it makes me pretty mad."

Just that will usually work. If not, she could say, "You wouldn't like it if I said that you didn't turn me on or you were bad in bed. I felt pressure to perform in bed to disprove you. Ken, you made me feel like a prostitute having to do sex acts that I didn't like." Rita eventually said she was so unhappy she separated from Ken and thought about divorce.

All of a sudden, Ken realized what he had done. He had been hurting her—and unknowingly was molesting her. Rita was so unhappy that she sought marital counseling because they were separated and were thinking about getting divorced.

All that news hit Ken hard. There was no way that he would in his wildest dreams have considered himself an abusive person, or that his abusive behavior was responsible for Rita's unhappiness. Ken started crying and told her very emotionally, "Oh, Rita, I am so sorry. I never meant to hurt you."

Rita realized that she, too, was responsible because she never told him her feelings. She could understand how he never picked up on her pain. She, too, was overwhelmed and could see how sincere his apology was. She, too, apologized for not being honest and for expecting him to read her mind.

The good news is that after Ken and Rita spent a few months in therapy, they reconciled their relationship, and they are still happily married. After several months of healing, Rita would occasionally volunteer to perform the sexual acts that Ken liked, even though they weren't her cup of tea. The difference was that she was doing them as an expression of love rather than psychological manipulation.

Others' Awareness of Our Patterns

What's obvious to others is often not obvious to us. Patterns are aspects of personality that are difficult for us to pick up on our own. When others point out our patterns, we usually smile and agree. Every time my wife and I watched "L.A. Law," I told her that Michael Tucker, who plays Stuart, and Jill Eikenberry, who plays Ann, are married on the show and are married in real life. I didn't realize that I told her this each time the theme music played. Finally, after about fifty episodes, she let me know about my pattern.

I thought about it and laughed. I said, "I guess I do, don't I? Why didn't you ever tell me this before?"

She told me that she got a kick out of the way that I said it the same way each time: "Did you know they're married in real life?"

Blatant patterns will be noticed by anyone (except the couple). Part of a therapist's training is piecing together overt and subtle patterns. That's why therapists and caring, observant friends can discover things about you much more quickly than you could on your own. If you're not happy but don't know why, therapy can accelerate the discovery process.

Therese went to a therapist because she was depressed about her latest breakup. She didn't understand why in the past few years, every relationship ended before getting serious. After telling her therapist about each man she dated, the therapist realized that she started talking about marriage exactly two weeks after each first date. Her reasoning was that she did not want to waste her time on a man who didn't want a long-term relationship, though she never knew she brought up the subject so soon.

She was scaring away a potential spouse by talking of commitment so early on. What she thought was fear of commitment was normal apprehension on the man's part. She called her friends and asked them when they began talking marriage. They all suggested she wait much longer than a couple of weeks, so she did.

If she had not gone to the therapist, she may never have known about her pattern. Therese's story does have a happy ending. Shortly after finishing therapy, she met Don and ended up getting married two years later.

In addition to our individual patterns, there are many scripts including parent-adult-child patterns, prejudice patterns, and rescuer-victim-persecutor patterns. They come to us from a psychological theory developed by Eric Berne, MD.

Parent-Adult-Child Patterns

Berne noticed that there are times when we are critical of behavior or instructive of others like a parent, are responsible like an adult, or act playful like a child. We get into a characteristic tone and mood in each of the modes. Let's look at them.

According to transactional analysis, when there's a balance among the three, our relationship with ourselves and others is healthy. However, when one of the three gets out of kilter, an imbalance occurs and relationships suffer.

Parent. Parents talk to their young children with a characteristic tone and directness. Parents know better and tell children what to do, what to think, and how to act. When children are very young, this interaction is appropriate:

> "Jimmy, you can have only one cookie."
> "It's bedtime."
> "Clean up your room before you go out."
> "You're going to start Sunday school."

As children grow into adulthood, parental involvement in their lives becomes less and less needed and appropriate. We're in the parent mode not only when we instruct or chide our children but also when we use the same tone and manner with others as if they're children. Here's an example of how one spouse relates to another in the parent mode:

> "You shouldn't have so many eclairs."
> "You should go to bed. You have to get up early."
> "Mow the lawn before you go out with your friends."
> "Don't sleep in. We have to go to church."

Spouses need to converse and exchange concerns as adults. Receiving a parental warning or scolding from an adult sets off the other adult. It isn't important that the adult talking like a parent may have some valid concerns (the lawn being mowed) or valid worries (getting enough sleep or not overeating). The message gets lost in the presentation.

Resentment kicks in, and three outcomes are likely. The first is that the receiver shuts off the parent for tone reasons alone. The second is that the receiver blows the parent's concerns out of proportion. When one spouse says, "Don't eat so much," the other spouse will think, *All that person does is hound me about what I eat.* A third outcome is to act like a child—go on an eating binge.

Adult. When adults deal with other adults, they do so as equals in intelligence, capability, and reason. Each values the other's needs and concerns. The essence of collaborative problem solving is adults inventing options that satisfy everyone's concerns. When people are spoken to in an adult manner, they respond like an adult. Here's how adults speak to each other:

> "Let me know what's important to you."
> "My concern is that we're making too many weekend plans."
> "Eat whatever you want. My concern is that you said that you wanted to lower your cholesterol. How can I be supportive?"

Child. Children are self-centered. Their jobs are to learn, explore, and have fun. Children tend to not understand why they can't have everything they want, and they feel bad when they don't get their way. A child's day is accentuated by great joy and marred by great sorrow, often within a few minutes of each other in a constant cycle.

If children want a whole cookie and the cookie breaks, they'll throw the cookie away, reasoning that no cookie is better than a broken one. They also don't have many responsibilities, which is good. Children say things like:

> "I want that now."
> "If you make me go to bed, I'll hold my breath."
> "I won't pick up my toys."
> "No! Mine!"

When children are told something they don't like, they tend to do more of that activity just to get a reaction. They also want attention. They want positive attention, but if they don't get it, they'll do things they know they'll get punished for because they figure that it's better to be yelled at than to be ignored.

If adults don't get the whole cookie, sometimes they'll want no cookie.

Harry wanted to see a movie. When he and his wife got to the theater, the flick he wanted to see was sold out. Instead of seeing another movie or doing something else fun, he was frustrated. He then threw an adult tantrum and informed his wife that they were going home. Their night was ruined, and they were going to be miserable.

When adults are spoken to as children, they act like children. Psychologically speaking, this is called *regression*.

Joyce tells Frank to stop watching TV and take the trash out to the street. Frank doesn't like being told what to do, and he thinks to himself, *Nag, nag, nag.* Even though he was planning to take the trash out in a few minutes, he sits on the couch eating potato chips, crunching them as loudly as he can.

Each time Joyce walks in, he makes a spectacle of finding a chip and ceremoniously putting it in his mouth. She gets upset, and he smiles to himself as she leaves the room. He is acting like a child in response to her acting like a parent.

Acting childish is contagious. He acts like a child so long that she becomes childish too. She says in a very nice way, "I'm sorry for nagging you. I'll empty the garbage. Why don't we go upstairs and make love?"

While they make love she has an orgasm, but she doesn't let him know. Then, before he climaxes, she rolls over and says, "I guess I'm really not in the mood tonight," and smiles to herself knowing that she is satisfied and he is frustrated.

Joyce and Frank have both regressed and are acting like children. The way to combat these feelings is for Joyce to realize when she's using a parental mode, and for Frank to realize when he is being destructive for destructiveness' sake. Also, Joyce needs to recognize when she is being pulled into Frank's trap and matches his destructive behavior with destruction of her own.

Prejudice Patterns

Prejudice is a very destructive pattern that manifests itself in many ways. Prejudice is another form of classical conditioning.

When we smell bread baking, for instance, most of us think of that as a pleasant smell. It kicks off our salivary glands, and we might even get hungry. Also, if there are positive associations with bread baking, we will recall them, and many of the physiological effects that took place during the fond memories will re-create themselves. It goes like this:

1. Bread baking
2. Smelling the bread
3. Getting hungry
4. Remembering Christmas when you had fresh bread
5. Feeling warm and safe
6. Smile and be happy reveling in the memory

Now, let's change the situation a little. Let's say that someone very close to you died by choking on a fresh piece of bread. That same olfactory (smell) response would trigger a whole other set of reactions. The beginning would be the same, but instead of feeling safe and secure, you would feel sad and resentful. Since every time you smell bread baking you feel bad, you eventually change your routine to avoid the smell. Then bread baking becomes repulsive to you as a protection from feeling bad about your friend's dying.

We're socialized to react certain ways when presented with certain stimuli. The stimuli change about every twenty years or every generation (which is why generations all have their own music, fashion, and hairstyles).

From a very early age, we have thousands of ingrained responses that set off a flurry of activity. When we are children, we decide some things that we like and dislike on our own, and for other things we rely on our parents to tell us what to like and dislike.

So let's say that you are marrying a bus driver. There is nothing in the world wrong with someone who drives a bus for a living. It is an honorable, well-paying, and highly responsible job. However, your parents are aristocrats, and the internal messages they have been receiving all their lives are that bus drivers are lewd ruffians who are unfaithful.

When you bring your fiancé home to meet your parents, what's happening in their brains is that they immediately process negative information about someone who drives a bus and they have a bona fide unpleasant response. The fact that they've never actually met a bus driver doesn't make any difference—the reaction is real.

Now let's say that your prospective mate is a pilot for an airline. The basic job description is the same—take people from point A to point B across the country. The difference is that being a pilot carries with it status. When people think of a pilot, positive feelings are the usual response. That same person would be greeted much differently—very positively—although the parents had never actually met a pilot.

These scripts are very powerful forces in people's lives and are not to be taken lightly. As in the example above, as much as the parents would want to like to have the bus driver as an in-law, it's very difficult for them. Understanding their positions can help detoxify the situation, but that's only a short-term solution.

In many ways, you handle this type of conflict the way you handle any conflict—understand the concerns and invent options. If the option parents, siblings, friends, or anyone else proposes is for you and your fiancé to break up, that is not acceptable. What you've got to do depends on their dominant functions (discussed in chapter 9).

In general terms you've got to break the script by having them realize that their perceptions about your fiancé are based on what they've been told to think. Give them permission to make up their minds based on what they think, not on what others tell them.

Rescuer-Victim-Persecutor Patterns

People also enter into the rescuer-victim-persecutor pattern. Let's investigate these roles.

Rescuer: I'll save you. A rescuer seeks people in trouble, and the focus of the relationship is the rescuer helping someone through a problem. A certain amount of rescuing is healthy and encouraged; it is a focus of Christian charity.

Rescuing becomes a problem when the rescuer takes on more than 50 percent of most problems. When people helping others are doing most of the work, it's a clue that there is overrescuing.

> Ben has been out of a job for two months. His wife, Sissy, types up his resumes, sends out letters, scours the help wanted section, presses his suits, and drives him to pick up his unemployment check and to interviews. She is putting in 90 percent of the effort in finding Ben a job.
>
> Though this might have been okay the first week he was unemployed, Sissy's rescuing Ben is actually adding to his difficulties in finding a job.

If you want to help someone but not be a rescuer, a good rule of thumb is to have the person put in at least 50 percent of the effort.

> Ben started taking some responsibility in finding a job. He would go through the help wanted section and get his interview suits ready. Sissy was better at using the computer and would type the cover letters and resumes, and she would take him to the interviews, so he didn't have to concern himself with the particulars of finding a job.

The reason her rescuing is making things more difficult for Ben is that it confirms his unspoken fear that he is incapable and incompetent—at interviews he comes across as lacking confidence.

When Sissy stopped rescuing and Ben took on the task of getting a job, he found one in three weeks.

Rescuing is a problem when the rescue is the focus of the relationship. Some people find others who are having a crisis. They want to rescue them, and working through the problem is the focus of the relationship. Maybe they have a drinking problem or a poor self-image, or they are recovering from a bad relationship. If that is the case, two events can occur. First, that relationship would continue longer than it normally would because of all the focus on rescuing the victim. Second, once the problem is solved, the maintaining force in the relationship is gone.

Rescuers often complain that their mates are being overly dependent. It's a kind of self-fulfilling prophecy. Rescuers encourage dependence by not allowing others to help themselves. When rescuers' mates allow rescuers to do too much or give up telling them to stop, they get accused of being dependent.

Victim: Rescue me. Victims are in relationships in which they are getting the short end of the stick. (Sometimes they are victims of violence or abuse, which I talk about in the appendix.) A victim seeks either a persecutor or a rescuer. Sometimes a victim has both, and sometimes only one. What does someone get out of being a victim? The concern and condolences of friends.

> Carrie frequently dated men who drank a lot and stood her up on dates. All the women from work constantly told her what jerks she dated and how attractive and intelligent she was and how she shouldn't be dating such losers.
>
> Though she didn't like being stood up, she did like all of the positive reinforcement from her friends. Carrie needs to realize that there are lots of ways of getting the attention that she craves without being in a bad relationship.

For couples who are married, the rules change. Victims need to tell their spouses that they don't deserve to be treated poorly. Victims should ask their mates how they would like being treated too.

Persecutor: I'll get you. Persecutors hurt people or relationships, usually for their own gain. Sometimes people are persecutors because others have hurt them and they are repeating the behavior. This happens frequently when people, especially men, were abused as children. (Abused women usually are abusive to themselves, or they put themselves in abusive relationships.) Other times people are abusive as a form of revenge.

In the fifty or so years spouses are together, there will probably be times when one or the other feels a desire to persecute the mate, either to retaliate for things the spouse has done or to use the spouse as a scapegoat for the horrible actions of others.

Riley and Marla have been married for five years. Any time Riley expresses his viewpoint, Marla verbally attacks him. She calls him stupid, or ridiculous, or says things like, "You have no taste whatsoever."

They are decorating their house, and Marla belittles each suggestion that Riley gives. Riley does not want to make the purchase of the new home a struggle, so he acquiesces to her every demand. In the end, none of the decorating reflects his tastes, and he is not happy with the home.

When you find a persecutor, like Marla, you'll always find a victim, like Riley, because persecutors need someone to attack.

Persecution is contrary to marriage vows. Persecution leads to escalation, and the end result is often abuse, adultery, or a breakdown of the relationship. Escalation gets messy because partners often forget the original reason they were mad at each other and focus only on increasingly hostile responses.

A persecutor needs a victim and can often find one. That's why in so many couples one partner has a hard style and the other a soft style.

Couples who find their relationship has a persecutor in it need to realize that it's not helpful. Doing collaborative problem solving as soon as concerns are developed will prevent escalation, which is the big danger in persecution.

Next, we'll look at pattern games. These patterns can affect our entire life. Sometimes couples have patterns that are so established they turn into a type of game.

PATTERN GAMES

Couples act out pattern games. Some of these games are fun, and some aren't. Each has players, goals, and rules. They resemble board games and can be very powerful forces.

Cross-Examination Game

Players. In the Cross-Examination Game you need to have a lawyer and a witness. Sometimes the person who plays the lawyer also pretends there's a jury and makes closing arguments.

Goal. To make the witness look as stupid as possible. To make the lawyer look as smart as possible, and to have lawyer, witness, and jury believe that the lawyer is 100 percent right and the witness is 100 percent wrong.

Rules. The lawyer, who is on the side of truth, justice, and the American way, questions and breaks down the witness. The witness must answer only the questions that are asked and only in the way that the lawyer wants to have them answered. If the witness is nonresponsive (doesn't want to play), the lawyer becomes belligerent.

How to win. To break down the witness and have her exclaim, "You're right, and I'm wrong. I throw myself at your mercy."

Common element. Asking people to define things. (Witness: "I'm not sure we're doing the right thing." Lawyer: "Define right thing.")

Outcome. There are three outcomes. Although this game is fun for the lawyer, it is belittling and degrading to the witness. The witness will usually avoid any confrontation with the lawyer so as not to have to "take the stand."

The second outcome is that the lawyer will be successful, and the game will be played until the end. The witness will say, "You're right, and I'm wrong," but will not really mean it. He just says that to stop the haranguing. Even if the lawyer is, in fact, right, the courtroom process will negate anything positive.

The third outcome is that the witness gets frustrated and walks out of the room, cries, or puts her hands over her ears. This is an example of a parent-child reaction (the lawyer being the parent, and the witness being the child). When people are treated like children, they can act like them. Kids puts their hands over their ears, and so do witnesses.

Remedy. If you are the lawyer, realize that you are not trying a case and that your victories are hollow. Also realize that you are alienating the person you are dealing with. If you do have a good point, it's being lost.

The cadence of the Cross-Examination Game is question, answer, question, answer in rapid fire. If you find yourself using verbal skills to manipulate or belittle people, stop and reread chapter 2.

If you are the witness, don't get caught up in the script. You may want to say, "It sounds like I'm being cross-examined. Are you asking me questions that way because you want to know what I have to say or to make me look stupid? I know you have some concerns, and I want to understand them."

Yes, But Game

Players. The Yes, But Game involves two players. Each can say, "Yes, but," or they can play separately. With each suggestion one player makes, the other counters, "Yes, but . . ."

Goal. To dismiss the other player's suggestions or criticisms out of hand so that yours are adopted.

Rules. Don't listen to the other party. While the person is talking, use the time to think of your next response or selectively listen to plan your attack.

How to win. Frustrate creativity and the other player, who gives up so the primary player can get his or her way.

Common elements. One person who thinks he knows everything about everything, and another who comes up with creative ideas and is supposed to look demure when constantly shut down.

Outcome. The person saying "Yes, But" wears down the person giving suggestions. The suggestor stops giving suggestions. The "Yes, But-ter" feels good about winning the round and smart because his superior intellect prevailed. The suggestor feels frustrated and angry at herself for allowing her good ideas to be bullied away.

Remedy. Ask if there's any suggestion that the primary player would consider. Also, you can break the yes, but rhythm by saying, "Let's be positive."

Darling Game

Players. There are two players in the Darling Game. It can be played by husband and wife, but also can involve parent and child, especially a daughter. (Example: "Don't be so stupid, darling.")

Goal. To say horrible, destructive things and then add the tag "darling" or "sweetheart." Saying "darling" afterward is supposed to negate the insult because it sounds loving.

Rules. The darling is not allowed to cry foul or feel hurt.

How to win. Get away with saying the meanest thing possible.

Common elements. The person saying "darling" feels that if she adds a nice coda, she can say anything. The "darling" is resentful, and does not feel darling at all.

Outcome. The darling feels badly and doesn't buy the game. The darling feels progressively worse about thinly veiled insults. The cumulative effect is resentment and hostility.

Remedy. Bring attention to the game: "The fact that you said 'darling' doesn't allow you to be awful to me," or "If you want to insult me, don't humiliate me, too, by saying 'darling,' which I take to be a term of affection."

Read My Mind Game

Players. The Read My Mind Game is usually played by two people, but the entire family can play. This is the favorite game of Introverts and conflict avoiders.

Goal. To have other players successfully guess what one player is thinking or feeling at any time.

Rules. One player has deeply held concerns, fears, desires, wants, or needs. He doesn't tell the other players what he is thinking or feeling. He can, however, give clues such as tone of voice, glances, or exasperated looks, or be difficult in areas not related to the concern. Mind readers must immediately see the clues and know exactly what they mean.

How to Win. The primary player wins by having the concerns unread for as long as possible. The penalty for not correctly reading the mind of the player is family disharmony. Mind readers win by correctly guessing what's on the player's mind.

Common Elements. The primary player is hurt at not having her feelings or wishes addressed. Mind readers get frustrated at not knowing what is causing the family disharmony.

Outcome. If the Read My Mind Game is played long enough, it can cause the destruction of the relationship. People can't read minds, and the "clues" that the primary player sends forth as obvious examples that he is upset may appear nonexistent, even to trained psychologists. Mind readers get frustrated and often have to guess by trial and error what's bothering someone.

Remedy. If the primary player is a strong Introvert, ask him about his concerns and wait ten seconds (see chapter 3). If the primary player is a conflict avoider, let her know that you can sense that something is wrong, but you can't read her mind. Ask her to share her concerns so that you can address them.

If you like to have your mind read, realize that the clues you are sending out that are obvious to you are not obvious to anyone else. Your mind isn't going to be read, no matter how miserable you make living conditions.

Say, "I have a concern about _____. When would be a good time to discuss it?"

PUTTING IT ALL TOGETHER

Patterns are common to any two people who have a close relationship. Patterns do not need to be destructive, but they often are. If you find yourself in a pattern, do what you can to break it so your relationship can proceed on an adult-adult level.

In the remainder of the book, we'll apply the personality and behavior traits for engaged and married couples. The next chapter is for engaged couples who might want to look at their engagement time as the start of where many of the successes and struggles in marriage begin.

Conflict Without Casualty for Engaged Couples

CHAPTER NINE

Getting engaged is exhilarating. The person you are most attracted to in the world and love dearly has just agreed to commit his or her life to you. All of a sudden you're faced with a flurry of decisions—when to have the wedding, who will be in the wedding party, where to have the reception, how many people to invite, and who to invite.

Later on, after the dust settles a bit, you have to start thinking about the nuts and bolts of your future life together. Decisions that may never have crossed your mind become real: How many children do I want and when? Where will we live?

During your engagement, you'll make some heavy-hitting decisions. There are thousands of opportunities to develop conflict resolution skills because that's how many joint decisions you'll make.

If you're reading this book before or while you're engaged, this book, and especially this chapter, will help you use your engaged time to set the structure for your future relationship together. If you're married, keep reading and compare your real-life experience so you'll know how well you did or why perhaps your engagement was rockier than you wanted it to be. Many marital problems started well before the wedding day, so tracing back to the roots can be a help.

In this chapter, I'll cover some of the emotional and intimacy issues that couples face concerning their new relationship.

IT WAS EASIER WHEN YOU WERE SINGLE

During the dating phase, you and your loved one enjoy vast resources. That doesn't mean you can take expensive vacations whenever you feel like it, but within your means you can pretty much do what you want when you want. The goal is to enjoy each other's company, learn about each other, and have fun. After a while, you add the dimension of sizing each other up for the permanency of marriage.

In *The Interpersonal Theory of Psychiatry,* psychiatrist Harry Stack Sullivan said that a person's greatest goal in life is to love and be loved.[1] He said it is the ultimate motivation of behavior. If you're contemplating marriage, you've been spending lots of time falling in love and loving your special person.

In the early dating stages, other than time commitment to each other and the level of sexual involvement, there are few places for conflict to get started, especially related to money. Feelings of infatuation and being on best behavior further reduce the incidence of conflict. But betrothal brings scarcities of one type or another. You also have the added complications brought on by members of both families, who have concerns and opinions of their own. Without collaborative problem solving, you're probably not having much fun. Collaboration turns conflict resolution into a challenge of inventing options to satisfy the needs of each person like a game with only winners.

YOUR NEW RELATIONSHIP

Engagement is a transition into a new type of relationship. In some ways it's an extension of dating, but in many ways it's far different. Let's take a look at some of the changes that you'll face.

One of the beauties of getting married is its permanence. That's essentially the reason for marriage. You give up your right to date whoever wants to date you, but in return you get the promise of lifelong companionship.

When you're dating someone and the person gets sick, has serious financial problems, or develops some annoying habits, or the burden is too much to bear, you have the right to leave the relationship. Marriage means giving up that right.

Some people think that the marriage vows are too restricting, but the reality is that the restrictiveness of the vows makes the institution work. My vows were similar to the ones many people take: for better, for worse, for richer, for poorer, in sickness and in health, to love and to cherish, forsaking all others till death do us part. Some couples fail to appreciate the gravity of what those words mean until they say them at the altar. The sentiments exchanged in the vows can help many couples through some rocky times if they remember what they promised.

An important part of *The Fight-Free Marriage* is discovering why you would want to be with someone you've known for two or three years for fifty or more. Maybe you've thought about it in general terms and even in specifics. Why are you getting married? What does that mean? How will your relationship change?

When two people find that they're getting married for the wrong reasons, it's a signal for them to think about their decision and put the brakes on until they've thought it through carefully. As painful as it is to end or extend an engagement, the future sorrow you avoid makes it well worthwhile.

Let's survey reasons that people get married.

WARNING: If you find that you and your loved one are unfit for marriage, you are encouraged to delay, postpone, or cancel the wedding until you can reach a collaborative solution. Many times you will be able to, but sometimes you will not. *This does not apply if you are a married. A married relationship is completely different, and I'll talk about what to do in this situation in the next chapter.*

WHY GET MARRIED?

One of the things I typically ask couples in seminars is why they got married or why they're getting married. Here are some of the results:

- love and companionship
- security

- to raise a family
- economic considerations
- safety
- to get out of an abusive home
- regular sex

Women answer with *raising a family* and *safety* more often than men do, and although few men say they want to get married for *regular sex,* almost no women have told me they get married for that reason.

To Have Companionship
Companionship is the number one reason that people get married, and it's a great reason. Still, everyone has a preferred level of companionship. If your partner prefers to spend every night with you, and you do, too, you'll need little tweaking. But that's not always the case. Often the preferred amount of togetherness differs. Joe and Ruth are thinking about getting engaged. Both are Extroverts, and each has a version of what togetherness means.

Joe likes playing cards with male friends three nights a week, and he spends Friday night playing basketball.
Typically, he and Ruth are together Saturday and one or two nights during the week. Ruth looks forward to the time together, but she is lonely other nights. She usually stays home and calls friends on the telephone. She wishes she could spend more time with Joe, but she figures that three nights are better than none.

Joe and Ruth are very much in love. Yet they cannot simultaneously be together, as Ruth wishes, and apart, as Joe is accustomed to. They've got to work this out before they get engaged.
In other situations couples want to be together, but they don't enjoy the time spent with each other.

Lorraine is an avid tennis player, and she likes playing several nights a week. When she and her fiancé, Sean, started dating, he wanted to spend as much time as he could with her, so he started playing. He thinks she looks great in her tennis outfit, and he loves watching her play.

Sean is new to tennis and still learning. Lorraine has been playing since she was twelve. As infatuation starts to wear off, watching her run around the court becomes less satisfying, so he accompanies her less frequently. He is starting to get annoyed at seeing her only a few nights a week. He absolutely doesn't like her always playing mixed doubles with handsome single men.

Lorraine is an excellent player, but not a very good teacher. She gets frustrated trying to teach Sean fundamentals, and her criticisms make Sean feel like a klutz.

Sean is concerned that he doesn't like staying home at night while Lorraine is playing tennis. She suggests that he do other things, such as join a bowling league. He says that he wants to be with her—and that's why he is marrying her.

The concerns. Lorraine's concerns are (1) to play tennis with people of similar ability, (2) to spend time with Sean, (3) to play tennis with Sean, and (4) to make Sean happy.

Sean's concerns are (1) to spend more time with Lorraine, (2) to allow Lorraine the flexibility to do things she likes, (3) to try to share her interest, (4) to not be bored at night, and (5) to make Lorraine happy.

The solution. Lorraine found out that her health club has courts available at lunchtime. Two days a week she can get to work early and play tennis during lunch. And getting a court on Saturday is easy if she makes reservations by Thursday.

Lorraine and Sean will take private lessons together from an experienced tennis pro skilled at teaching. She can learn advanced techniques while he learns fundamentals. This solution satisfies all their goals. Lorraine finds that playing in the middle of the day is great and makes work go by a lot faster. After getting to spend most nights together, Sean has realized that his jealousy was unfounded. Everyone is happy.

To Raise a Family

Raising a family is a good reason to get married. But you still have lots to think about. For instance, the child-raising part of your life is only about twenty years. The primary husband-wife relationship needs to be enough after the children are grown and gone. And there are other considerations: How many children would you like? How soon after marriage will you start having them? What type of birth control, if any, will you use?

Robert Burns said that "the best laid schemes of mice and men are often led astray." Anytime you have sex, even with every type of birth control available, there is a possibility of pregnancy. Women do get pregnant on the honeymoon! Are you prepared for the responsibilities of parenthood soon after you get married?

> A newlywed couple were talking about their five-year plan. They were going to save up money for two years, live off one income and save the other for three years, and then begin to try to have a baby.
>
> Although they didn't know it at the time, as they were talking about this intricate five-year plan, they were already expecting their first child. The five-year plan got adjusted.

To Enjoy Sexual Intercourse on a Regular Basis

Many people get married so they can have a sexual partner. A lifelong sexual partner is certainly one of the benefits of getting married. Sexual intercourse serves four functions: (1) to have a sensual experience (sex can bring pleasure to all five senses—touch, taste, smell, hearing, and sight—as well as the thrill of orgasm), (2) to communicate love and feelings of emotion from one person to another (that's the intercourse part of sexual intercourse), (3) to feel desirable as a sexual being, and (4) to have a baby.

In the thousands of times you'll make love in your life, you might experience two or three times in which all dimensions are simultaneously met: your body finds it perfectly satisfying, you're able to communicate total love to your spouse, you feel that you are desirable to the opposite sex, and you conceive a baby. Most people never achieve all four dimensions of sex at the same time.

Sex has several goals. God invented male and female bodies to be complementary. Couples who get married only so they can have sex in marriage with an attractive person will quickly find that anything done hundreds of times will lose its magic if the main concern is personal gratification. Let me be very blunt. Though it's a wonderful part of marriage, having sexual intercourse regularly is not a good reason to get married.

Sometimes distressed couples who are getting married primarily for a sexual partner are being pushed into marriage by both sets of parents. The parents feel uncomfortable with their children's sexuality. This is especially true for women. Many parents find it very difficult to see their adult daughters as sexual beings. If you are in this predicament, discuss this issue with your parents.

Parents don't want their unmarried daughters to get pregnant. Part of that is stigma, and part of that is genuine concern for the daughter to not have to endure the rigorous realities of unplanned parenthood. Parents also know that the father of the child of an unmarried woman is likely to renege on his responsibilities, compounding the problem.

The pregnancy argument worked until the 1960s, with the invention of the birth control pill. All of a sudden, the pregnancy issue changed dramatically. Of course, women on the pill solved some problems and created others. The first is all of the side effects of the pill. The second is that sometimes the boyfriends and husbands of women on the pill assume that because they can't get pregnant, they are perpetually ready, willing, and able. The third concern about the pill is moral; some couples have concerns about any kind of artificial birth control.

If you feel that you are getting married because your parents are uncomfortable with your sexuality, you need to address the issue—and fast. Don't get married to please any person other than you and your fiancé. I would suggest having your minister or a trained counselor present to help you out.

My wish for everyone is that they not try to make themselves into anything that they're not in order to fit the mold that others have made for them.

To Have Someone Make You Happy

Many people are not happy. They're lonely or depressed, or they don't know many people. They get married so that the mate can make them happy. This is *not* a good reason to get married.

Someone else cannot make you happy for a lifetime. That's something you have to do on your own. Someone else can sweep you off your feet or temporarily fill a need. Here's what Geena had to say:

> I had been alone in a remote New England town for over a year. My job took me there, and I didn't know anyone. I didn't have a date for over six months, and I gained ten pounds. I didn't feel attractive, and my life was miserable.
>
> When I met Craig, he immediately took my breath away. He thought I was the most beautiful girl he'd ever seen. My life all of a sudden became exciting and wonderful. Two months after meeting him, we got engaged. I know it seems a little impulsive, but I don't think I'll do any better. I mean, Craig adores me.

Craig and Geena were engaged for about six months. They didn't stay married long enough for their first anniversary.

If you're getting married to fill in a puzzle piece that's missing in your life, that should send out a zillion signals to you to wait.

I know that tens of thousands of couples out there meet and marry within a year and everything works out fine. Still, when you do this, you're making your job very tough. Save yourself some heartache. A good rule of thumb is to date for about a year and a half just to make sure that you're not infatuated, and to try to be engaged at least a year.

To Be Rescued or to Rescue Someone

As I mentioned in chapter 8, some people have a strong need to rescue others, and they may get married to fulfill a script.

Other times, a loved one may be in an abusive family, and the individual wants to take him or her away. But rescuing someone by marriage will provide only a short-term solution.

Rescuing or being rescued is not a good reason to get married. Someone from an abusive background can make a great spouse but usually requires extensive therapy first. You are much better off to discover other collaborative methods for protecting someone and keeping him or her safe.

WHY NOT GET MARRIED?

What do you do if you discover that you are getting married for the wrong reasons? Reconsidering your marriage plans may be the wisest move you ever make.

After you've told all your friends, and your wedding day has been the focus of many people's lives, having second thoughts may seem out of the question. M. Scott Peck in *The Road Less Traveled* says that we distract ourselves from the importance of the wedding ceremony with all the trappings because if we realized what we were doing—pledging our lives to someone for life—most of us would be traveling very fast in the opposite direction from the church.

You may go through with it because so many people have made such huge efforts to be there, and you feel obliged to them. You may also be concerned about what people will think or the nonrefundable money that people spent. Maybe you're just not comfortable with such an intimate, private decision to be made public. Maybe you don't want to embarrass yourself, your loved one, or anyone else. Maybe you feel guilty about upsetting the lives of so many.

Put all your fears to rest. If you call off or delay a wedding, others won't look at you like you're from Mars. Family and friends, if they truly care about you and your future, will be very understanding.

Read about Mia's situation:

Mia moved from San Diego to Anchorage and fell in love with Jim. They decided to get married, and they had lots of friends and relatives coming to the wedding. If you have ever traveled to Anchorage, you know that it's expensive and time-consuming to get there.

Two weeks before the wedding, Jim told Mia that he wanted to give up his job as an engineer and live off the land in an igloo in the wilderness. Mia, who is a strong Extrovert, decided that type of life wouldn't be for her.

She called off the wedding even though many people had bought nonrefundable airplane tickets and most of the reception expenses were also nonrefundable. She wasn't going to spend her life with someone simply to save face. (By the way, she still had the party, and though she was too upset to attend, all the guests had a great time!)

Not one person said anything negative to Mia, and years later, she has no regrets.

BETWEEN DATING AND MARRIAGE

Your new relationship brings other concerns too. Engagement means you're not exactly dating, and you're not yet married. This is an in-between time. How couples handle this strange, though usually short, time can have profound positive or negative effects on their married years.

Sexual Intimacy

Reconciling sexual urges before marriage with the desire to be true to one's faith and values is a hot topic among engaged Christians. As a therapist to whom people honestly share intimate details of their life, and as one who teaches undergraduates at Rivier, a small Catholic college in New Hampshire, and Boston University, a large metropolitan university, I know what's happening in the world.

This subject must be treated gingerly because anytime an opinion even slightly more liberal or conservative than our own is expressed, strong feelings are invoked. As a therapist, I need to be respectful of a couple's faith so I asked representatives of the major Christian denominations their views on sexuality. What I quickly discovered was that Christians do not speak with one voice on this issue. One common thread is that every denomination views marriage as the appropriate venue for sexual intercourse. However, if we put physical intimacy on a continuum from holding hands to making love, there is a wide variety of opinions on how couples can manage their feelings of desire for each other.

For instance, many denominations view masturbation as an acceptable outlet for sexual desire, but others view it as sinful.

There was little agreement about the appropriate pastoral response for couples who are sexually active before they get married. The Episcopal Church, for instance, has two officially sanctioned premarital programs—one for couples who are sexually active and one for couples who are not. The Episcopal view is that dealing with the subject openly is the best way to provide pastoral care, while other Christian denominations are deeply offended by what they feel is a sanction of morally illicit behavior.

As a therapist and an author, it is my job to respect the views of my patients and readers. If patients' views are more liberal or more conservative than my own, I do not try to force my views onto them because that would be parental and my therapeutic approach is adult-adult. Remember, the goal of therapy is not to make people carbon copies of me, but to help them make decisions that are best for them emotionally, practically, and spiritually.

Because sexuality issues and a person's faith are so intertwined, let me give you the advice that I give to couples who I see in my practice.

How to Proceed

The advice I pass on to couples is this: (1) Realize that many of the intimacy problems that married couples face start before their wedding day. (2) To resolve these issues, talk to your minister about the subject of sexuality and get his or her views on the subject that are consistent with your faith. Ministers talk about sexuality issues every day and are great sources of spiritual direction. You will find that priests and ministers will provide information that is godly, practical, and in your best interests.

Sexual intimacy gets a lot of press, and one, but certainly not the only, function of sexual relations is intimacy. (Even newlyweds, who experience the lifetime height of sexual activity, only make love five to ten hours out of a 168-hour week.)

What Is Intimacy?

Though sex is one way to express intimacy, there are many types of intimacy in a relationship. Just what is intimacy?

Intimate relationships are an important part of being human. Babies who have no other human contact will die. The most severe form of punishment, even for hardened criminals, is solitary confinement. When God set up marriage, he intended for us to have an intimate human relationship with one person of the opposite sex. That intimacy begins at engagement, and often does not reach its peak until decades later.

Intimacy is a way of communicating how much you love someone. When couples are in love, they want to share special times with each other. They exchange personal secrets that they would not tell to another person. Intimacy can make people feel special, wanted, and vital.

One of the most intimate moments in our life is when we get engaged. What each person is telling his loved one is that I find you attractive—physically and intellectually. I want to make love with you thousands of times. I want you to be the parent of my children, and of all the people in the world, you are the one I choose to share my life with.

That level of acceptance of who you are inside and out is awesome. It is the beginning of stronger, closer bonding.

Intimacy lets you know if someone can be trusted. Intimacy brings vulnerability. When someone respects your values and innermost thoughts and feelings, it is a signal of how much someone can be trusted. It is a strong measure of how much that person values you and your relationship.

Intimacy can help you find out if your partner is interested only in a superficial relationship. If your girlfriend is not interested in true intimacy, then she might be telling you that dating is her preferred level of relating and that engagement is not appropriate.

Intimacy is a positive aspect in our lives. However, sometimes too much of a good thing can be destructive. Let's look at this aspect of intimacy.

Reasons to Limit the Amount of Intimacy Before Marriage

Too much too soon can harm a relationship. Lionel and Mary have been dating for three months. Each enjoy the other's company, and they are having fun. Lionel has shared many personal secrets and thoughts with Mary, but she is the type of person who is very private.

She is increasingly becoming anxious when Lionel tells her details of his life that are very personal, while she has no intention of opening up to him.

During dinner one night, Lionel tells Mary that he loves her. She tells him that she is flattered, but that she's not looking for such an intense relationship. Lionel is crushed, and they never see each other again.

This is a classic case of too much intimacy too soon. Any time one member of the couple wants more intimacy than another, it is the member least interested that controls the destiny of the relationship.

Intimacy can make you feel that you are in love. The feelings that intimacy invokes are powerful. Exposing yourself emotionally makes you very vulnerable, and having someone respect that vulnerability and give you complete acceptance invokes very powerful, positive emotions that can best be explained as a feeling of euphoria.

This feeling is nice, but it isn't love. Many couples think that they're in love and later discover that they were only extremely attracted to each other.

Ministers will tell you that the toughest part of their job is officiating at the marriage ceremony of a couple who is wildly infatuated and is getting married impulsively. It's like there's an elephant in the room and everyone notices it but them. Friends and family telling them to slow the process down just strengthens their resolve that their love will see them through.

What they're feeling are strong emotions of intimacy, caring, and self-worth—many times these emotions are greater than any they have ever experienced. While these emotions are wonderful, they're not love. Ideally, they should be cooled off before couples get married, but they're often not.

Sexual intimacy can be physically dangerous. Sexual intimacy shares many of the characteristics of other forms of intimacy, with the exception that not all sexual relations are intimate—some are pure recreation. What Hollywood doesn't tell us when they show couples who meet and immediately jump in the sack (a practice that rarely happens these days in real life) are the physical downsides. Sex is a very powerful force with consequences that can create a human being. Most married couples look at having a baby as a blessing, even if the timing is not the best. Though it happens over a million times a year, most unmarried mothers will tell you that being a parent without a husband is no fun.

Another subject that is very important to consider is getting AIDS. I don't want to be hysterical, yet there are hundreds of thousands of single heterosexual people each year who get HIV or AIDS. Very few of them thought it would happen to them, so as unpleasant as it is for many people to think about, accurate information is the key to stopping the spread of this disease.

The following data comes from the Center for Disease Control. We don't want to think of our mate as a potential disease carrier. He or she is loving, kind, attractive, and well-groomed. Also, the type of activities that lead to AIDS can be a bona fide expression of love. Infatuation tends to blind us to negative evidence about our mate, and the fact that she or he may be a disease carrier is certainly something most of us don't consider.

Here are the facts: (1) AIDS is a virus that invades our bodies. It doesn't care about someone's physical attractiveness or how much you love someone. (2) Anyone who has had oral, vaginal, or anal sex—or shares needles—is at risk of contracting the virus. (3) Anyone who avoids these activities cannot get the virus. (4) HIV is a virus that precedes AIDS. Although HIV is not deadly, HIV will always change itself or seroconvert to AIDS. (5) There is no cure for AIDS. *If you get it you will die from it.* (6) Using a condom greatly reduces, but does not eliminate the risk of AIDS. (7) People tend to not mention high-risk behavior to new partners for fear of scaring them off. (8) One person in a hundred has had sex with both men and women within six months prior to a heterosexual relationship. (9) Four percent of men and women surveyed, single and married, have reported having sex with someone other than their partner in the past year.

What this means is that if you are absolutely, positively, certain that your partner has not participated in a risky behavior for six months and has tested negative on an AIDS test, then you're protected from infection. Two people who are not infected cannot infect each other. (The exception, of course, is the extremely unlikely event that people could contract AIDS through tainted blood. Now that blood banks are aware of the problem, incidents of people contracting AIDS from a blood transfusion are virtually non-existent.)

If you have any questions about AIDS, you can call the Center for Disease Control toll-free, twenty-four hours a day. The people who monitor the phones are well-trained and talk about all forms of sexuality many times each day. Your call is confidential, and the information that they give to you is accurate. *Their phone number is 1-800-342-AIDS.*

According to the Center for Disease Control, the only absolutely safe practices of sexual intimacy are (1) kissing (theoretically French kissing can transmit the HIV virus, but it is unlikely); (2) holding hands; (3) hugging and caressing; and (4) masturbation (of oneself). The CDC does not want to be alarmist or have men and women avoid each other. However, since a monogamous, committed relationship is the only place any form of sexual expression can take place without fear of contracting AIDS, couples need to think very seriously about putting themselves and their partner at risk.

BUILDING THE LOVE NEST

Many couples decide to live together before they get married. But I can tell you from a conflict resolution standpoint, living together is a disaster.

Again, in an attempt to present both sides on an issue, here are reasons that people give for living together.

Living together gives you a taste of what marriage will be like. It will give you a taste of what having a roommate of the opposite sex is like, and you do get to see your potential mate in nondating situations.

Living together in some ways provides a taste of marriage, and in other ways it does not. Individuals in this living situation still guard and control their resources and possessions. Many times they are anxious about bringing up concerns that they feel would damage the relationship because in cohabitation, the partner could

144 The Fight-Free Marriage

leave on a whim. That's why the divorce rate for couples who live together is not significantly different from couples who choose not to live together before marriage.

Living together takes away the stress of just being married because you've eased into the transition. Newlyweds have lots of stress for many reasons. Changing where you live, your commute to work, where you go to the supermarket, and so on can be stressful.

Two can live cheaper than one. I know this is arguing by fortune cookie, but my last fortune said, "Whoever said that two can live cheaper than one lived alone."

Here are reasons why living together is not a good idea.

You're on best behavior. This is probably why, statistically, couples who live together don't stay married longer than those who don't. People psychologically sweep problems with the live-in partner under the rug. When they get married, they realize, often for the first time, that if they don't say anything, they will have to live with an annoying habit forever. The frustrations of living together may come out all at once.

Brenda and John lived together for four years. John used to live in California, and he frequently called friends there. His phone bill averaged two hundred dollars a month. That always bothered Brenda, but she didn't feel it was her right as a girlfriend to comment on how John spent his money.

After they got married, John called all his friends to thank them for wedding presents and talk about the honeymoon. The phone bill came back a month later for six hundred dollars, even though they were trying to save for a house and a new car. The frustration Brenda felt came out all at once: "If you didn't spend so much time on the phone, we'd save thousands of dollars a year."

John was taken aback: "You never mentioned this before."

"Well I'm mentioning it now," she responded angrily.

Both felt hurt and anger as raw emotions were stoked.

We can also be on best behavior in other ways. No matter what is bothersome, the tendency is to be outwardly supportive but inwardly upset.

Living together can be too much closeness too soon. Living with someone before marriage may bring the relationship to an intensity and closeness that it can't handle yet. Two people who would be perfectly suited to marry after three years may find the relationship leaking at the seams if they move in together after two or three months.

The taboo part of living together can artificially sustain a relationship. This is true especially if family members don't approve of cohabitation. The feeling that they are perpetually doing something sinister can artificially sustain a relationship.

People are not protected in unexpected circumstances. According to laws of many states, if people don't take the responsibilities of marriage, they don't get the benefits. Couples who live together for extended periods of time may acquire furniture and possessions or even have children together. Bank accounts and shared bills get very messy if the relationship breaks up.

Depending on the state, a breakup can cause major financial problems. Courts won't handle issues like child support, custody, and visitation. In short, each person is at the mercy of the other.

Engagements typically last a year or two. It's important to find the right amount of intimacy and closeness that nurtures the relationship, keeps your spiritual values, and provides a solid foundation for your next fifty years together. The biggest mistake couples make is they use engaged time like marriage.

Intimacy is an important part of life. When men and women are falling in love, they want intimacy to be at its highest level to nurture the relationship and to promote feelings of self-worth. Besides, being intimate with our love feels nice.

Engagement time is an in-between time for couples. How couples handle intimacy in the year or so they are engaged will have a profound effect on the rest of their lives together. Intimacy is like a two-edged sword. Too little can weaken a relationship while too much will stress it. Since engaged couples are planning to spend the rest of their lives together, it's appropriate for them to find a level of intimacy that lies between dating and marriage.

In finding that level, couples need to candidly discuss what's right for each member and for them as a unit. When discussing sexual intimacy, the conversation needs to cover the following issues: (1) What is the appropriate expression of physical desire as it relates to each member's values and faith—keeping in mind that all Christian denominations view marriage as the appropriate venue for making love; (2) the costs versus the benefits with an honest discussion of issues such as pregnancy, disease, as well as negative effects of any type of intimacy.

Living together before marriage is another common aspect of American culture. Again, it's natural for couples to want to be together. Still, engagement time is an investment in the future, and couples who live together tend to not develop the conflict resolution skills they'll need in their married life.

You'd think that with societal values pulling them in one direction and Christian values in another, all the intimacy issues to work out, and planning an entire life together, there wouldn't be a moment to spare from the "Will you marry me's?" to the "I do's."

However, many couples plan a ceremony and a reception afterward that take up an enormous amount of time, money, and energy. Since it's such a huge investment, let's take a closer look at the Big Day.

ISSUES CONCERNING THE WEDDING DAY

"I wish we had eloped!" is often bemoaned after a wedding by bride and groom. What's intended to be a happy occasion can often be marred by people getting over their heads in cost or complexity. Every wedding isn't tragic or strenuous, but it seems that every wedding has its tension-causing moments.

After the couple get engaged, the standard operating procedure is to set a date, talk to their clergyperson, then look for a place to have a reception, line up a photographer, listen to music demo tapes, pick bridesmaids and ushers, and so on and so on.

All the hubbub surrounding the trappings associated with a marriage can be fodder for honing conflict resolution skills or the stuff nightmares are made of. To complicate the problem, if the getting-married experience has left you parched, you must now face married life with few of the skills you'll need to make your new lifestyle fun.

Money, Guest Lists, the Ceremony, the
Reception—and Other Issues

Many times after a wedding there is a party. There are all kinds, of course. As a guest, I've had a wonderful time at an elegant, but understated reception at the church hall in a small Tennessee town. I've also been a guest at a New York wedding that easily cost over fifty thousand dollars, which is a huge amount of money for what essentially is a party. *Bride's* magazine estimates that the average cost of a wedding reception these days hovers around sixteen thousand dollars. Wow!

I had always dreamed about my wedding day. I would be like a princess, pampered and lavished. I wanted everything to be perfect, and even if we had to run our credit cards to the limit, we'd have our whole lives to pay it off.

The financial decisions that you and your beloved make are your own business and no one else's. Still, shelling out sixteen grand for a party is a huge chunk of change. Dropping that kind of cash for one day's fun is bound to be a breeding ground for conflict—and it is.

I was so relieved after the wedding was over. It seemed that all Tony and I did was fight.

Having other people provide the cash does not eliminate conflict; it just shifts to different types. Every wedding guide I've ever read says to parents, if you're paying, sign over the check, and let the couple spend it the way they want. But that's not usually how it goes.

Father: Oh, the things they wanted to do were horrendous. I wanted a classy affair. I was inviting my best customers, and they wanted a circus. I forked over four months' salary for them, and they have the gall to redline my guest list. Well, that was the last straw.

Son: He wanted to run everything. We wanted to have a simple reception in a tent in the backyard and invite all of our friends. His guest list included people we don't even know, leaving no room for our friends.

And then you can run into the problem of disparate resources or people clinging to traditions.

Jim: I'm paying for this wedding, so it's going to be run my way. I'll allow my daughter a little flexibility on the wedding ceremony and certain parts of the guest list. If she wants things her way, she can pay for them.

Fred: Business hasn't been very good this year. I want to make this a special day, but I really have only ten thousand dollars to spend. My prospective son-in-law's family wants a more elaborate reception, and I understand they have only one son. I can't afford it. I would be mortified if they paid for a more extravagant wedding. What would people say?

Matt: These are the nineties. Who says that I should have to pick up the entire wedding tab? My son-in-law's parents are better off than I am.

Each situation must be handled differently. In each case, focus on the concerns of the people involved, and focus on your own concerns.

The wedding industry will try to tell you the amount you spend on a reception is a sign to the world how much you love your spouse. Ridiculous! It's the wedding ceremony that's a sign of how much you love your spouse.

- All of the shoulds and musts that you hear are coming from the wedding industry and need to be taken with a grain of salt. You want to have an elegant wedding and a nice reception. And you want your guests to have a good time. Also, getting dressed up in special outfits like flowing gowns and tuxes is fun. (Every woman wants to wear a wedding dress.)
- You're inviting friends and family who know you and like you. Much of the wedding industry will tell you that your job is to impress the socks off them and supposedly try to convince them you are of the aristocracy. If people need to

be impressed that much, perhaps they don't belong on your guest list. (But don't worry. I've never met anyone that superficial.) The tactic of many unscrupulous people in the wedding industry is to use fear, uncertainty, and guilt: "You get married only once," "Obviously, this day isn't important to you," or "What will people think?"

- Don't sweat the little things. (A corollary to that rule is that they are all little things.) People can work themselves into a state because of the seemingly minutest of issues. Usually, there is a conflict about the way something "should" be done when the reality is, there are no shoulds.

At Laura and Frank's wedding, both mothers picked out blue dresses. Laura's mother didn't care what anyone else wore, but Frank's mother didn't think it was appropriate.

Frank's mother made a big stink about it and made all of the prewedding events tense and uncomfortable. Neither would give ground, and five years after the wedding, the two still don't talk.

A great book to read is Abigail Van Buren's *Dear Abby on Planning Your Wedding*. It covers all of the sensitive issues and gives wise resolutions, and it has a balance between practical and lavish. She offers many useful ideas on how to have a special wedding in every situation and for every budget.

Inventing Options Is the Key
The key to enjoying the wedding is to keep in mind the goal of sharing a sacred event with your closest friends. Then have some fun at a party. Invent options until everyone's concerns can be met, which they will be. Put your personality into your day. It will be special, and you'll avoid a cookie-cutter wedding.

There are many ways to be creative. Here are a few:

- Two pharmacists who were getting married sent their invitations in pill bottles.
- One couple paid for fifty people to fly from Boston to Florida in February for the weekend. The charter cost one hundred

fifty dollars per person for a total of seventy-five hundred. Each hotel room cost fifty dollars for Saturday night. They needed forty rooms for a cost of two thousand. They got married at a church and then went back to the hotel. Guests were on their own for Saturday and Sunday and went back home on Sunday night.

Everyone lounged by the pool while back in Boston it was below zero. The total cost for the reception, which everyone will remember forever, was under ten thousand dollars. (And the hotel chain where they stayed let them stay free for a week anywhere in Florida for bringing so much business.) Here are just a few creative, cost-cutting wedding ideas.

- Use goldfish as a centerpiece.
- Hire a disc jockey instead of a band. At Ringo Starr's wedding, there was a Beatles reunion. That's probably been the only time a wedding reception band didn't sound the same. With a disc jockey you have control over the quality of the music.
- Provide a karaoke machine instead of a disc jockey.
- Serve a selection of hors d'oeuvres instead of a sit-down meal. Most restaurants cannot prepare many meals to be served at once with much quality. People love Swedish meatballs and scallops wrapped in bacon. (P.S. Figure on eight hors d'oeuvres per person as a rule of thumb—most hotels charge about a dollar to a dollar fifty per hors d'oeuvre. P.P.S. I was talking to a rabbi who officiated at the wedding of many Hollywood stars, and he told me that in Tinsel Town it's the height of chic to have hors d'oeuvres receptions.)
- Have a barbecue with outdoor games.
- Have a potluck, and ask people to bring food as a present.
- Take guests to a baseball game or play.
- Place disposable cameras on each table.
- Have your wedding cake as the dessert.

You're making the transition from singleness to marriedness with a partner you love dearly. There is one overriding way to make your engagement fun.

MAKE YOUR ENGAGEMENT FUN—
THINK AND TALK ABOUT BEING MARRIED

Many couples spend a small fraction of time thinking about the marriage because they're overwhelmed by making preparations for the ceremony and reception. But you're getting ready for the most exciting ride of your life. It's common for both of you to have worries that you keep to yourselves. Talking about them will help. Also, certain issues are bound to crop up during your engagement that you'll have months to work out. This will keep your first few weeks of marriage as unburdened as possible.

You've got no shortage of things to think about. Where you're going to live, how many children you'd like, the type of birth control, if any, you'll use, and budgeting are starters. Exactly how life will change and how you can avoid many problems that couples encounter after marriage can be next. Talk about your joy, but also talk about your apprehensions.

This chapter we looked at engagement. Engagement is a time of investment for couples. Therapists know that couples who make an easy adjustment to marriage used their engagement time to learn about each other.

We also know that many struggles couples face started long before their wedding day. Making the transition from engaged to married is wonderful. Next chapter will look at the issues newlyweds face, as well as "oldyweds."

Conflict Without Casualty for Married Couples

CHAPTER TEN

After you and your beloved have been declared husband and wife, kissed, had a party, gone on a honeymoon, got back to your new home, and the bride's been over the threshold, it's time to begin your life together.

MARRIED LIFE IS DIFFERENT

Your relationship with your spouse is different from that with every other human being. This relationship is sacred, and it is a promise from God that if you don't give up the two of you can find happiness together.

No matter what the circumstances of your marriage, even if they haven't been the best, you'll find that there's a way for both of you to be happy together. Your job is to figure out how. It all gets back to the concept of covenant.

In this chapter, we'll take a look at Conflict Without Casualty for newlyweds and then for couples who have been married more than a year or two.

CONFLICT WITHOUT CASUALTY FOR NEWLYWEDS

It is an unfortunate fact that many couples separate two years after their vows. Many of the couples who do stay married regard their first year together as stressful. But it doesn't have to be. Couples who use Conflict Without Casualty principles find that much of the difficulty can be lessened.

We can see from couples who have a rocky start that the fairy tale of newlywed bliss is a myth. Though reality can never compete with fantasy, all couples can be happy together.

Forget About the Myths

After you've crossed the threshold, forget about all of the myths you've heard about marriage. Nuptials don't guarantee that everything will magically fall into place. You have to be an active participant in your marriage. First of all, any life change brings stress. Couples who've lived together report that there's still lots of change to deal with. (Premarital cohabitation is not a panacea for elimination of marital stress or adjustment difficulties.)

If you used your engagement time for conflict resolution skill development, newlywed time will be much easier. If you didn't, you can't change the past. You can, however, start to use the principles of Conflict Without Casualty at any time in the relationship.

Some challenges that you'll contend with are (1) money, (2) household chores, (3) misunderstanding of opposite gender habits, (4) sexual adjustment, and (5) parenting.

Money—Yours, Mine, and Ours

Unless your last name is Rockefeller, you are bound to have money problems when you first get married. It doesn't matter how thick your bankbook is. No matter what age you get married, financial responsibilities stare you straight in the eye.

When couples get married in their twenties, they're just starting their careers. Their income potential is at its beginning stages, and there are lots of things to buy (dishes, a refrigerator, cars, bigger or nicer living arrangements). Some couples want to start a family, which means a bigger house, day-care expenses, a possible drop in income, plus all of the child's expenses (food, diapers, clothes, and medical care).

When couples get married in their thirties, they're making more money, but they often want to start a family right away. Each partner may have a career that's developed and personally fulfilling. Couples in this age range may want to move from an apartment to a house, they may need bigger accommodations or a new car, or they may start saving for retirement. These situations require much discussion and collaborative problem solving.

When couples get married in their forties or later, they may have children from a previous marriage, and even though they've hit their stride as far as income potential is concerned, they have children's college and other expenses.

The bottom line is that no matter when you get married, money is tight. A person's income potential is generally not reached until late forties or early fifties when the house is paid for and the kids are out of college.

Watching your parents spend money and being told all your life financial shoulds and shouldn'ts have influenced your view of money. These parental messages are very strong, and even when they're contrary to your values, you may have an internal conflict without knowing it.

For instance, some adults have heard all of their lives that they should never have a credit card. Others have heard all of their lives that it's foolish to carry around cash, and they should have a credit card for large purchases. This is what can happen:

Meg: I think we should get a credit card. I don't like going into the city with cash. [That's what her parents told her.]

Bryan: No. When you have a credit card, all you do is buy things you don't need and can't afford. [That's what his parents told him.]

Meg: I'd pay off the balance each month.

Bryan: That's what people say, but it's very easy to get hooked.

Meg: That's stupid. Are you calling me irresponsible?

Bryan: Are you calling me stupid? I just don't think credit cards are a very good idea.

Meg: I think they're a good idea.

And so on. Meg and Bryan are arguing over positions. Actually, their parents are arguing in absentia. Because of that, Meg and Bryan find it difficult to support their arguments because they aren't truly committed to their positions; they just have an inner voice telling them to keep the family truths.

The gist of the conflict is that Bryan, when he was younger, always wanted to have a credit card, but he always needed a cosigner and knew his parents wouldn't do it. Bryan is arguing positions he doesn't really believe in.

People argue their parents' positions long into adulthood. Usually, it subsides after their parents die, but sometimes their parents' voices keep ringing from the grave.

The key to knowing whether parental voices are speaking is to listen for the word *should*. *Should* is a parent word. Here are some examples:

> "We shouldn't spend so much money."
> "People should be considerate of others."
> "Men should be the ones in charge."
> "Children should be seen and not heard."
> "A mother should be with her children."

Though the conclusions may be your own, the use of *should* is a signal that you're advocating someone else's values. What you should do (just kidding) is analyze what you're saying and do some soul-searching. Are these your values as an adult? Why or why not?

Bryan and Meg's solution was to obtain a charge card with a special feature. When they used it, the money came directly out of their checking account.

A big transition from single life to married life is what to do with money as it comes in and goes out. When you are single, you have control over your own domain; you can spend your money as you please. If you don't have the money, you can charge your purchase.

When you are married, that all changes. Each couple has to work out what is best for them. Here are the problems: (1) You've got two people with different ideas about how money is best spent or not spent, and (2) you have different income levels, which may be close or not close at all.

Personality-Type Characteristics

Personality types tend to have common views on spending and saving money and acquiring possessions. Here are the tendencies.

Sensing/Judging (SJ). Sensing/Judging types tend to like traditional values, delaying gratification, and saving for a rainy day. No matter how much money they have, they're very careful with it. They tend to avoid risks.

Even when they have a lot of money, you might never know it. Rich Sensing/Judging types live comfortably in middle-class neighborhoods. The only difference between them and their neighbors is that they have lots of money in federally insured bank accounts and bonds.

Even before they've hit their stride, Sensing/Judging types will be very concerned about life necessities being taken care of first. They'll be vigilant about all bills being paid on time, especially the rent or mortgage and car payments. Using car money or house money for play will not be greeted kindly.

Intuitive/Thinking (NT). NTs are very good at problem solving. They're willing to take risks because they feel they can problem solve their way out of any fix.

The dilemma is, problem-solving skills can take one only so far. Also, being Intuitives, NTs tend to not be concerned with details, and they get involved in projects or investments or buy products that aren't fully researched. They quickly find out that details that didn't interest them turn out to have been vital.

Intuitive/Feeling (NF). NFs are typically not concerned with money. They want enough to live a comfortable life, and they want the spouse and family to be happy. NFs tend to spend extra money on family or travel, though Extroverted NFs run up huge phone bills.

Because they aren't concerned with accumulating large amounts of money, you'll often find them in human service positions making far below what their work is worth. NF types may be librarians, social workers, or psychologists or work in other helping occupations.

Sensing/Perceiving (SP). SPs just want to have a lot of fun. They like to experience all that life has to offer. They live for the moment and spend for the moment, though they'll save for a trip, a car, or a boat. SPs tend to make a lot of money as surgeons or relatively little money as mechanics or police officers.

When different types are married, which is usually the case, conflict is built-in. For instance, if Sharon (an SJ) marries Andy (an SP), they are going to have very different outlooks on money.

One of the reasons couples with different personality types get together is that they complement each other. Sharon gets someone who is spontaneous and cares about here and now. Andy gets someone who would put some money in an IRA.

Now that they're married, Andy wants to take extra money and buy expensive toys. Sharon wants to save for a rainy day, knowing that the house will need to be painted next year.

Let's say that Andy and Sharon both worked overtime and together have an extra $500.

Andy: We should spend the money on a new Sega system. [Sharon doesn't like that idea because she knows there will be household expenses down the road.]

Sharon: We should put the money in the bank for the house, which we know will need painting next year. [Andy doesn't like this idea because he thinks it's boring. He wants to play the latest video games. Besides, he thinks that if they can have an extra $500 now, they'll get it again sometime in the next year to take care of painting.]

They need to find out how much each costs. Andy looked through the paper and made a few calls and found that Sega costs $200, but the games cost $50 each. Sharon called around and got estimates on the housepainting, which would be $500. The painters felt that their house could hold out for another year before painting became necessary.

They agreed to buy the Sega master unit but to rent games from the video store for $2 per night. Andy could have a variety, and if there were any he liked so much he would want them more than twenty-five days (the cost of $50 in rentals), they'd buy them when they had enough money saved to paint the house.

They would take the other $300 and put it in the bank. It was agreed that Sharon would be in charge of this money and it would be used only to paint the house.

After Andy got the Sega system, he noticed that games were being sold in the want ads and at garage sales for only about $5 each. He bought a couple that way, and after they had saved for the painting, he bought several more.

Money and Control

When one partner has control over money, it can create resentments in the other spouse. The controlling spouse can resent the time it takes to make decisions and payments. She also doesn't like always having to lay down the financial law. When couples have this problem, they need to realign the responsibilities.

When they do it by type, they can handle monetary responsibilities in ways that are good for everyone. How would you divide responsibilities? Here's what Sharon and Andy did:

Sharon handles all the car, health, and life insurance they pay as well as their rent and car payments. Sharon makes sure these bills are paid on time, and she feels good that all the big items are taken care of.

Andy buys food and his clothes and he pays for entertainment. He enjoys researching, window-shopping, and testing products as well as actually purchasing them.

Each has money for gas and daily expenses like lunch.

They are happy about getting to spend money the way they like.

Living Conditions

When a male and a female build a love nest together, one of the things they quickly find out is that it doesn't clean itself. That's a shame, too, because life would be so much easier if it did. Assuming that you and your spouse don't have enough extra money to hire a housekeeper, you have to figure out who does what and when.

Couples who figure this out solve a big part of the roommate side of marriage. Ineffective dusting is not grounds for divorce in any state! Still, different expectations or skills in chores can add stress to and steal joy from your marriage.

If you and your spouse are both neat freaks or you're both willing to live with clutter, you've got it made. An imbalance can mean trouble. But there are solutions to help you out.

A major complaint of women is that they're socialized to be the housekeeper, whether they stay at home or work outside the home. (Radio commentator Paul Harvey said the best way for a husband to seduce his wife isn't by giving flowers; it's by cleaning the bathroom.)

The power base in chores goes to the person least concerned about them. Sensing types tend to be much more aware of dirt and clutter and therefore more concerned with housework than Intuitives are.

Jamie and Rick have been married three years. Jamie doesn't like dust in the house, and she spends a good amount of time vacuuming and dusting. Sometimes she gets really busy and asks Rick to dust. He looks around the house, doesn't see the need, and tells her so. She usually gets exasperated and says, "Will you just do it?"

Rick acquiesces, turns on the TV, and dusts the furniture tops, but most of his attention is on championship wrestling. The first few times Jamie checks up on him, he dusts like a banshee, but after a while of feeling like there's a hall monitor in the house, he reduces his efforts to a few token swipes with the feather duster.

Finally, Jamie can't take it anymore. She grabs the duster out of his hand and says, "Forget it. Just watch wrestling. If you don't want to help me, I'll just do it."

This is their pattern concerning chores, be it dusting, washing dishes, or cleaning the bathroom:

1. Jamie does the cleaning.
2. When she is busy, she asks Rick to clean.
3. Rick thinks things are fine and cleans what looks dirty, but not what he can't see.
4. Jamie checks up on him.
5. Rick feels like he is a child.

6. Rick lets Jamie know he's not interested by giving a token effort.
7. Jamie takes over, but makes Rick feel bad.
8. Rick feels bad and does something fun to give the appearance he doesn't care.
9. Jamie withdraws; Rick withdraws.
10. The next day they pretend nothing happened.

This pattern is repeated time and time again. It's like a script, and each knows his or her part. They need to (1) get rid of the script and (2) figure out ways to resolve this conflict collaboratively.

Neither Rick nor Jamie is happy with the current situation. It needs fixing. When Rick was single, he kept his apartment spotless and organized, which isn't exactly front page news. Single people are on their best behavior. It's part of the mating game, and it keeps the human race going. Can you imagine what it would be like if you knew everyone's secrets on a first date—be it overflowing hamper or other bad habits? There would be very few second dates!

Jamie often laments that she was tricked because she thought that Rick was neat, which isn't really fair to Rick.

Misunderstanding of Opposite-Sex Habits
Marriage brings a spouse and simultaneously a roommate of the opposite sex. Since we're on best behavior before we get married, visiting a potential spouse at their bachelor or bachelorette pad isn't the same as moving in together.

Newlyweds suffer through all the typical roommate difficulties: "Why do you keep the heat so high—our electric bills are out of sight," "The radio is up too loud," "I want to go to sleep early," "The alarm wakes me up too soon," "You snore," "Do you really have to get up in the middle of the night to go to the bathroom?" and on and on.

But there are differences between newlywed roommates and the roommates you had before you got married. For example, if you didn't get along with a roommate, you could get another one at the end of the lease. Couples read over their marriage vows, and it hits them that the lease is up when one partner dies, which—God willing—is a very long time.

Here is one of the more intriguing cases I've encountered of a couple who had difficulty adjusting to opposite-sex habits:

Paula and Quincy had been married for six months. Both were twenty-four years old. They were seeking therapy because they decided that they had to end their marriage, though neither seemed particularly enchanted with the idea. They had lost all hope and were coming to therapy as a last-ditch effort.

I asked them why. They told me they couldn't afford a bigger apartment, specifically one with two bathrooms. After listening to them for a while, I learned that the crux of the problem was that she didn't like whiskers in the sink, and he didn't like nylons hanging over the shower.

My standard operating procedure is to review the wedding vows, and we decided together that this situation fit under the "for worse" and possibly the "for poorer" categories. I helped them work on their problem together.

Paula's concerns were that she didn't like stubble in the sink. It made her ill to use the sink afterward, and she didn't want to get near them to clean up. She said that she always put her nylons over the shower curtain. That's the way her mother taught her to do it, and it never bothered anyone else.

Quincy's concerns were that he had to get up before Paula, and even though he tried to clean up the sink, being perfunctory at 5:30 in the morning was tough. Also, even if there was one whisker in the sink, she treated it like it was radioactive waste. As far as the nylons were concerned, he said that they were cold and clammy in the morning and he didn't like dealing with them.

The problem needed collaborative problem solving. The solution, like most solutions, was relatively simple.

Quincy bought a large supply of plastic basins from a hospital supply store and put one in the sink. After he finished shaving, he put the basin in the trash. He got to shave and the sink was hairfree. The cost of the solution: five cents a day.

Paula found that there are other ways of drying nylons. Since her mother suggested many years before to dry them over the shower, I asked her to ask her mother for some suggestions. Her mother said to wrap them in a towel and put the towel in the closet.

Both problems were solved. Paula and Quincy stayed married, and they are very happy together.

Sexual Adjustment—Great Sexpectations

The media constantly barrage us with images of perfect sex. Madison Avenue works hard to convince us that all we need to do is buy a panoply of products and sexual gratification will result.

Two common events can creep into the newlywed bedroom. The first is that couples have physical difficulties of one type or another. Impotence, cystitis, difficulties achieving orgasm, painful intercourse, pregnancy, and premature ejaculation are very real possibilities. None are mentioned in the myth of perfect newlywed sex.

Fortunately, all, except pregnancy, can be treated medically. There are effective therapies for male dysfunction like premature ejaculation and impotence. Cystitis can be cured with antibiotics. The pain of intercourse can often be eliminated with over-the-counter lubrication. Talk to your doctor candidly about any type of sexual problems. Don't be embarrassed or ashamed. Doctors deal with sexual difficulties many times each day, and they can help with any problem that you have.

An old story reports if a couple puts a bean into a jar each time they made love their first year of marriage and then took a bean out of that jar each time they made love after the first year, the jar would never be empty. There's an old Italian expression, *Non e' vero, ma fa un bel conto,* which means, "It's not true, but it makes a good story." Still, it's perfectly natural for couples to be in high gear when they first move in together. It's also perfectly natural for passion to continue until a couple's diamond anniversary and beyond.

The legitimacy and normalcy of marital sex is unnerving to some couples. Instead of their having to steal away for a tryst, everybody knows they are having sex, and no one cares.

Guys used to brag to their friends about their sexual exploits, but they quickly find out that no one cares how far they got with their wives.

Louise's mother-in-law wanted a grandchild. After a long and involved interrogation, Louise cracked (yield-lose) and told her mother-in-law her menstrual cycle. Each month she'd call Louise on her fertile days, and she'd tell Louise to call her son for a baby-making session. Louise knew that her mother-in-law knew she was making love, and that didn't make it very fun.

When Louise and her husband, Kris, went to her parents' house, her mother would make their bed and say that she'd look really cute in the nightgown Aunt Edna gave her from Frederick's of Hollywood.

Newlyweds often experience reinfatuation. They want to please each other and enjoy the thrill of having their love in bed with them each night. After a few anniversaries, new concerns develop.

God made us sexual beings. He wants marriage to be a lifelong commitment between two people who enjoy a healthy sex life.

Sexual Variety

A foundation of marriage is the "forsaking all others" part of the wedding vows. Sexual variety is possible in a monogamous relationship, but couples vary in their need for it.

When couples are happy with the expectedness of sex, there is no problem.

> Betty and John have been married for twenty years. They both like making love in their bed every Friday night after the monologue on the "Tonight Show." They look forward to it and find it quite pleasurable.

When both spouses want to try new things in new ways and in new places, there is no problem.

> Wilma and Jake have been married for fifteen years. They like making love outdoors. Their goal is to have sex in each of the fifty states and at least five continents by the time they're seventy.

But there can be frustration when one partner craves variety and the other doesn't.

Melissa and Peter have been married for five years. Melissa likes making love with Peter, and she wants to experiment a little. Peter finds comfort in making love the same way each time. Melissa is starting to get a little bored and is finding her mind wandering during sex.

One night, Peter came home to see candles burning in the dining room and Melissa lying naked on the table with peanut butter strategically placed on her body. She handed him a couple of crackers and asked him if he wanted a peanut butter sandwich.

He was really turned on and wanted her to go upstairs. She refused. She told him that he could have sex with her there or not at all. When he countered with a no of his own, she told him that she couldn't believe he was passing her up.

In therapy they talked about that night. He said that he wasn't raised to treat sex like an animal does. She said, "I'm your wife. Live a little."

Melissa and Peter's situation is common when one partner wants variety and the other doesn't. The issue can be the sexual position, the type of lovemaking (like oral sex), the place, the time, or whatever. If Melissa wants to have a man lick peanut butter off her body and make love with her on the dining room table, she's got to do it with Peter, or wait until Peter dies and try her luck at marrying someone from Shady Acres Nursing Home!

The most common reason for the spouse to seek the status quo is a feeling of awkwardness. Sometimes he has parental voices ringing in his head about what proper behavior should and shouldn't be. (If Peter asked his parents, which he never would, whether they thought it was okay to make love to Melissa on the dining room table, they'd probably say, "Sure, that's where we conceived your brother. You're married. Whoop it up!")

First of all, we have to decide what is normal behavior for married couples in a monogamous relationship. As a therapist, I can tell you that there is no normal. As long as no one is being manipulated or getting hurt, physically or emotionally, normal is whatever makes the couple happy.

When it comes to sexual variety, I can guarantee you that friends of yours practice sexual activities that you think are reserved only for romance novels. People tell their therapists things they don't even tell their best friends.

When it comes to sexual variety, conflict resolution is like other resolutions—with the exception that you have to wade through all the muck of what you've been told all your life is "proper" and "improper."

Here are some questions to consider when deciding how comfortable you are with adding to your lovemaking repertoire:

1. Is the activity consistent with your marriage vows? Sometimes men have a difficult time reconciling a wife in her roles as mother and as a sex partner. Some men have been told that there are two types of women—mothers and women who fool around—and they can't separate the two roles after a baby is born.

This can leave wives sexually frustrated because their husbands don't want to have recreational sex with them anymore. Couples who are in this predicament need to realize that a woman's sexuality as a generally accepted concept has only been around for about one hundred years.

The voices saying that mothers cannot be sexual beings go back hundreds of years ago when orgasm for a woman was thought to be a welcome call for demons. Women weren't supposed to have orgasms so that they could remain demon-free during conception and gestation.

Now that we understand sexuality better, we know that orgasm is a healthy, natural part of life and that dividing women into the two classes of those who have offspring and those who don't isn't good for either the wife or the husband.

2. Does one partner of the couple have strong moral convictions against the activity? A husband wanted to videotape their lovemaking. His wife didn't mind as long as the tape was immediately erased. She had strong convictions that she did not want anyone other than her husband looking at the tape, even accidentally.

There is little consensus among Christians on what is morally offensive. Some consider masturbation, either alone or with a spouse, sinful, while others view it as morally acceptable form of sexual sharing.

There's disagreement on many forms of sexual positions in marriage. When missionaries first went into Africa many years ago, they were shocked to see Africans making love with the woman on her hands and knees and the man behind her. The missionaries thought that was animalistic and preached the only "godly" form of sexual expression for a husband and a wife was the husband on top, the missionary position.

Others would say that any way a penis gets into a vagina in a monogamous marriage is by definition holy. It's the act, not where the participants are facing, that's important.

3. Do you find the behavior offensive? Preferred sexual behaviors differ from person to person. Just as someone may like classical music and artichokes, another may like rock music and ice cream.

Oral-genital sex is an activity that many like both receiving and giving, either as a warm-up to intercourse or as an activity in itself. Many people like only to receive or only to give. Others like neither.

If someone doesn't like this activity, it doesn't mean they're sexually broken. Some people like ice cream and others don't, but you won't find people feeling badly about themselves because they don't like Rocky Road.

It's never appropriate to coerce someone into sexual behavior considered offensive. It's always appropriate to stop doing anything sexual the minute you find something disagreeable.

Jenny is a twenty-two-year-old newlywed. She likes performing oral sex on her husband, but she doesn't like receiving it. She knows she's "supposed" to like it, but she doesn't. [There are no supposed to's in sex, any more than there are supposed to's in anything involving personal preference.]

Ramone is thirty years old and has been married for nine years. He feels guilty because his wife performs oral sex on him, and she has asked him to do the same to her. He doesn't want to. He believes that the vagina is unclean. [Actually, genitals of both sexes are very clean, especially for women.]

Heidi is forty-five years old and in her second marriage. She objects to the idea of oral sex and doesn't want to participate in any way.

The problem is that Jenny's, Ramone's, and Heidi's spouses can't participate in an activity they like. Nevertheless, anytime someone finds an activity objectionable, it's not appropriate to force it. People change. It's appropriate every now and then to test the waters and see if the idea is still objectionable. Sometimes when a person gets more comfortable with the mate, certain behaviors are more appealing.

4. What would the worst case be? You may make love in a position that isn't satisfying to you (or you may love the new position). You may feel silly. There may be voices telling you that's not a proper activity. (This is different from breaking strong moral convictions.) If this is the case, try to decide what you want apart from what others tell you to want. This is especially true when no one but your spouse needs to know about your sex life.

5. Try things on a small scale. If, and only if, the four criteria above are met to your satisfaction, you might want to try some variety. Start on a small scale, and work toward your goal.

For instance, when people have a fear of flying on an airplane, they don't strap themselves in a 747 and take off to London.

They start off in a class and talk about flying. When that's okay, they watch planes fly. Then they listen to the sounds of engines. Then they go to an airport. Then they sit on a plane. Then they taxi onto the runway. Then they take a short flight. The technical term for this is *systematic desensitization*—proceeding to the next step only after you are comfortable with the preceding one.

The opposite approach—strapping someone with a fear of flying into a plane and taking off—is called *implosion*. Sometimes implosion works like a charm, and other times it doesn't. If it doesn't work, the participant has an anxiety attack, and may not want to repeat the experience.

In sexuality matters, where people are very vulnerable, implosion is too chancy. You're much better off taking things one step at a time so partners can ease into an activity they're feeling anxious about.

Peter didn't have any objections to participating in Melissa's dining room table fantasy. The worst case is that he would feel silly and have to clean peanut butter off the carpet.

The first night, she was on the table, and he put peanut butter on her. Then they ran upstairs, showered, and jumped in bed.

The second night, he licked the peanut butter off her and then stopped.

The third night, after licking the peanut butter off her, they began making out on the table and finished upstairs.

The fourth night, they planned to start making love in the dining room and finish in the bedroom. Melissa had an orgasm soon after they started, and Peter was so excited that he did too.

Peter decided that he liked making love in different places and watching Melissa get excited. He began to love Melissa's creativity. One night when she came home from work, he answered the door naked, and they made love on the stairs.

Melissa found that her boredom ended, and she once again enjoyed making love with Peter (in bed and out).

When You Want to Be Parents

Another source of joy—and conflict—in a marriage is having and raising children. Sometimes one spouse wants to have a baby, but the other doesn't. Other times both spouses want a baby, but they aren't able to have one. About one in seven couples is unable to conceive.

Gynecologists, urologists, and fertility experts can provide couples lots of assistance if one or both spouses are having trouble with the conception. Fertility treatments may be covered by insurance too. If you have concerns in this area, talk to your doctor, and he or she can give you specific advice and make recommendations.

If it turns out that for one reason or another, even with the help of modern science, you cannot conceive a child, an issue remains: Which is more important, to be parents or to have a baby? Hundreds of thousands of babies and children in the world need loving parents. Adoption isn't a sloppy second. Ask children of loving adoptive parents whether they feel any less their children, and they'll tell you no.

Some parents seek out a child with their physical characteristics so that it will seem more like their child. That is certainly a personal decision. And I can tell you that American parents who have adopted children of other races and countries love them as their own.

If you've thought about adopting a child but don't know where to begin, ask your priest or minister. You may want to start with the Catholic Relief Organization or some other agency for counseling and assistance.

Once couples become parents, other problems can crop up. They may have completely different parenting styles or wishes for their kids.

Parenting Styles

Often a couple learn to get along with each other, and the relationship cruises on autopilot. Then one day the pregnancy test is positive, and the couple learn they're about to be parents. The conflict resolution patterns are about to change big time.

The biggest mistake couples make is to assume that life will be the same after the baby is born, except they'll be parents. Wrong. In therapy most of what goes on when new parents are having problems is convincing them that life could not possibly be the same with their new bundle of joy.

Nowhere is the fallacy of relating to others the way you want others to relate to you more prevalent than when parents relate to children. Children may or may not have the personality type of their parents. Also, in only about one couple in fifty do both members have the same personality type. This dynamic can create all sorts of friction. Each of the personality areas, if they're different from those of the parents, will be looked at with a jaundiced eye from the child who doesn't understand or appreciate his parents, or the parents who assume the child has their same type. (There is no correlation between the personality types of parents and that of their children.)

Use the information in chapters 3 through 6 with children and you'll find parenting much easier. Children can learn collaborative problem-solving skills as young as two. Be their teacher and they'll be good students.

Conflict Resolution Style

Conflict resolution style has two components. The first component is the child's style. As was mentioned in chapter 2, children learn how to solve conflicts from their parents. Kids will repeat both constructive and destructive patterns.

The second component is the way the parents deal with each other in regard to the baby. Sometimes they compromise and each feels put upon every time there is a compromise. Other times parental instinct will take over. The person who was very acquiescent in dealing with others will suddenly be a tiger when issues concern the baby.

I'm a strong believer in maternal instinct. If a woman believes that her children are in danger, she is likely to dig in her heels and not give in one iota.

The good news is that when couples understand collaborative problem-solving skills, they'll find that collaboration on baby issues is the same as on other issues.

Parents Don't Have to Be Awful

Some parenting advisors advocate humiliation, harsh punishment, physical cruelty, and awful tactics to make children cave in to their wishes. They think cruelty when kids are very young is the key to stability as an adult.

Families are always pleasantly surprised when they find that Conflict Without Casualty works with children too.

The American standard is for parents to resolve conflicts behind closed doors so they can show a united front to the children. This approach isn't good for the parents, and it isn't good for the children, either. It isn't good for the children because their best opportunity to learn collaborative problem-solving skills is from their parents, and if they never see parents solve problems, they have no idea how to do it.

Conflict resolution behind closed doors is not good for parents because it can be very stressful. Also, in appropriate situations parents don't have the advantage of having the kids help in solving problems. Here's an example:

Mary was concerned that her fifth-grade son, Eddie, was not doing his chores and that early evening TV watching left him too tired to do his homework. Eddie's chores were not overly burdensome; he had to empty the garbage. Mary and her husband, Clark, spent countless times arguing about what to do about their son.

Clark thought that Eddie's grades, usually Bs and Cs, were okay, and that the price of higher grades would be a boring childhood. He knew that Eddie didn't do his chores every night, but Clark would empty the trash when Eddie didn't.

"You're just teaching him that if he's not responsible, then you'll do his work," Mary said. "And I know that if he did his homework first, rather than watch TV, that he would be getting As and Bs."

Their arguments were blights on their lives. Clark and Mary didn't want any more children for fear of what more stress would do to their marriage. Both parents choked out a half-baked compromise when Eddie was around as an attempt to show a united front.

Eventually, Clark and Mary knew that when they were alone, the subject of what to do about Eddie would come up, and the cycle would begin again. They would change their routine so that they wouldn't be alone while awake in their bedroom. One would stay up longer than he or she wanted to and get up earlier than necessary. Their sex life had become nonexistent.

Finally, they agreed to do collaborative problem solving with Eddie. Here's how it went:

Mary: Eddie, I have some concerns. My concerns are that the trash gets too full, and homework done later in the night doesn't get the right attention.

Clark: My concerns are that fifth grade is a time when you should have some fun.

Mary: I agree.

Clark: Really?

Mary: Of course, I never wanted to admit that because I felt that would weaken my position.

Clark: Eddie, what are your concerns?

Eddie: I really want to watch *Star Trek: The Next Generation.* That's right after dinner. If I empty the garbage, I'll miss the part when they say, "Space—the final frontier." Besides, I spend an hour every night doing my homework.

Mary: So your concerns are being able to see your show.

Eddie: Yes.

Clark: What if we taped your show and you could watch it after your homework? If you start your homework at seven, you can watch your show after you're finished. During the commercials, you can empty the trash. If there's no time to watch your show during the week, you can stay up late on Friday and Saturday nights and watch it then.

Mary: This would address all of our concerns. What about yours?

Eddie: If I start my homework at seven and don't finish until nine, it will be too late for dessert.

Mary: Okay. If you're still doing homework at 8:15, then you can take a dessert break. Does this sound good?

Afterward, Clark and Mary stopped avoiding each other and started enjoying each other's company again.

No matter what hat couples are wearing—parent, spouse, or family member—they can use the same collaborative skills.

CONFLICT WITHOUT CASUALTY FOR MARRIED COUPLES: KEEPING THE FLAME BURNING BRIGHT

Next we'll look at issues that couples who have been married for a while have. There's no clean definition for when couples make the transition from newlywed to just plain married because it doesn't happen on any particular day.

The most frequent reasons couples have problems are that one or both spouses avoid conflict and don't know how to deal with anger or concerns. Little problems can have a cumulative effect. Other times people start feeling taken for granted, and sometimes the responsibilities of being a spouse or parent sap joy from life.

Here are some general strategies for staying happily together and making the most of your relationship.

Date Your Spouse

I know in New Hampshire spousal dating is legal, and I'm pretty sure that is the case in all states. One of the common complaints that therapists hear from couples is that they are so caught up in daily living that they don't date anymore.

When people are single, they like to make the most of their time together. Both members of the couple will be dressed to kill. Every detail is carefully considered.

Then the couple do something special together. Holding hands and making out at red lights are optional. While they're out on their date, they enjoy each other's company as they share the experience.

Everyone looks back on the premarital dating time as fun and exciting. If the couple hadn't thought dating was fun, they would have started to date others.

Dating your spouse is a simple, yet incredibly powerful way to revitalize a relationship. Not only do you start relating to each other as a couple in love and not as parents or roommates, but as Masters and Johnson put it, "The best foreplay happens with your clothes on."[1]

Before offering dating tips, I'd like to mention excuses couples give for not dating. The two most frequent excuses are (1) we have no time and (2) we have no money.

Time is a precious commodity. Both spouses may be in the workforce, and there are kids to take care of and baby-sitters to find. You have to think of something to do, get there, and get back. And then the budget enters into the equation. Even with all of these realities, by using a little imagination and ingenuity, you can overcome each and every one of them.

First of all, you have to find a fun place for your kids to go during your date. Couples don't date with their offspring. This is couple time, not parent time. If you have a regular baby-sitter that you can afford, great.

Perhaps you can explain to your day-care provider that you and your spouse need to spend some couple time and ask if one day a month you could pick up your kids a couple of hours later. The person will likely say yes.

If money is tight, go to friends and neighbors and relatives you would trust with your kids. Talk to them about a swap. Say that you and your spouse want some couple time, and ask them whether they would be willing to take your kids for a night if you take theirs for a night. Chances are, they'll love the idea.

Dating with Shallow Pockets

You don't need lots of money to date your spouse. There are many kinds of dates too: the fun date, the seduction date, the celebration date, the elegant date, the participatory date (Rollerblading), and the vegging date (watching a play or movie). When you have some extra money, blow a little on each other. Even when your pockets are shallow, you can have a night-on-the-town date, let's say at the Ritz Carlton, for $10.

Putting on the Ritz

Part of dining in a restaurant is the experience of getting ready, going to the restaurant, and having linen tablecloths, sterling silver cutlery, and five waiters in tuxedos. The $30.00 steak you get at a fancy restaurant is good, but it's not that much better than the $7.95 one you get at a family-style restaurant.

Also, when you go to a restaurant, you are often so satiated by the time you get to dessert that you pass it up or don't enjoy it fully. How can you go to your favorite restaurant and spend $10? Just order dessert or coffee.

You can still call and make reservations. You can still get

dressed up in your favorite clothes. The woman can wear jewelry and nylons; the man can wear cologne. (If you don't have perfume or cologne and want some, go to the mall and use the testers.) When you get to the restaurant, you can still say, "We're the Smiths. We have reservations for two." Jacques, the maitre d', will still say, "Very good, sir and madam, come right this way." In short, you get the entire experience of going out on the town.

It doesn't matter that your main course was Hamburger Helper at home. You are now dating in grande style. If you just order coffee or dessert, both can be served for $10 at any restaurant in the country. If you're not on such a tight budget, you can order the appetizers too.

Feeling types will wonder, *Won't the restaurant manager get mad and yell at us?* (See chapter 5.) After having worked in restaurants for many years, I can assure you that couples get just coffee or dessert or appetizers all the time. It's a very chic thing for the upper crust to do after shows or the ballet.

Tell the host or hostess that you're just having coffee or dessert. You'll be seated with a waiter who is handling a party of eight and can't take a table with a full meal. Or you'll be seated at a table of someone just starting as a waiter. You'd be the perfect training table.

Putting on Howard Johnson's

If you don't feel like going to a fancy place, the ambience and atmosphere of going out can be achieved just as easily at a local chain restaurant. It doesn't really matter where you go. What matters is that you and your spouse feel special and spoiled. I suggested going to a fancy place every now and then because women frequently lament that they don't get to dress up and go out anymore. And both men and women like seeing spouses all decked out.

If you're wondering what to do, try some of the dates that you enjoyed before you got married. You thought it was fun then. Who knows? You may think it's fun again.

If you need more ideas, go to your library and talk to the

librarian. Say that you are looking for fun things to do on a date with your spouse. (Many librarians are Intuitive/Feeling types so they'll naturally have many ideas and like the idea of spousal dating.) You'll choose from a long list of dates in every price range, including no-cost ones. The library may even offer passes to museums, parks, and other places.

Look in the paper, talk to friends, or use your imagination. Once you get your creative juices flowing, you'll find lots to do.

Dating Tips

There are a few dating guidelines. The first and foremost is that for a few hours, you're a couple. Your kid's failing math, your dog's having fleas, and your leaky roof will all be there tomorrow for you to tackle. Kids and family problems are taboo subjects during the date.

Another common lament is that the spouse doesn't listen. In fact, this is the root cause of most divorces. Many listening problems can be traced to differences in the Introvert/Extrovert preference and the Sensing/Intuitive preference (see chapters 3 and 4).

Dating can provide the forum for listening. Much of what some therapists do is listen to their patients. People feel safe in therapy to talk about themselves. If the issue isn't serious, a spouse can take the place of a therapist and not charge eighty dollars per hour. All of someone's feelings, fears, hopes, and dreams won't come out on the first spousal date, however. Regular dating allows time for couples to talk, to share, to laugh.

Millie's dream was to be a sculptor. She was an accounting major in college because her parents said that if they were going to pay thousands of dollars a year in tuition, they wanted her to be able to get a job.

She worked as an actuary in a big insurance company and made over sixty thousand dollars per year. Still, she wanted to go to art school and learn to be a sculptor. She knew deep down that she had talent, but she never had training.

Millie knew that even top sculptors make only a fraction of what actuaries make. She and her husband, Arnie, were trying to save for a house, which was important to her.

She kept this dream locked up inside and was quickly becoming resentful of her job and her marital commitment, fearing that they were keeping her down.

When she came to therapy, I asked her if she had shared her dream with Arnie, and she said no. She was afraid that he'd get mad or think she was stupid. When I told her that her being angry with herself for being in a job she hated was harming her marriage, she decided to tell Arnie.

One time when they were dating, she told him. He wanted to help her pursue her dream, but he was concerned they would have a loss of income. He had known her for five years, and she had never given him an inkling that she was interested in being an artist.

With his support, she enrolled in evening art classes. Eventually, she worked at the insurance company four days a week and sculpted two days a week and in the evenings. Knowing that being an actuary didn't cause her to lose her dream, she started enjoying her job.

After they started dating, Millie and Arnie found that they were both married to interesting people. Before, by the time they got home, had dinner, and turned on the TV, they hadn't given themselves time to listen to and appreciate each other. Now they look forward to their dates.

A common question is how often to date. It depends on each couple and their responsibilities. I would think that dating once a month is a minimum. If you can handle once a week or more, that's even better. Dates can be just a couple of hours or a whole day or evening. It's up to you. An important part of any relationship is to make dating a high priority.

Have Friends Other Than Your Spouse

Therapists ask couples whose relationship is hurting, "Who are your friends?" They may point to each other and say, "He is," and "She is," and that's it.

It's important to have same-sex friends to share interests that your spouse doesn't have. It's also important to have other couples as friends. Opposite-sex friends don't have to be a problem, but they can be. Sometimes when a member of a couple is having marital difficulties, the boundaries between a married person and an opposite-sex friend can get mushy, and that mush can lead to adultery, especially if the opposite-sex friend is filling a dating void or a listening ear in the stead of the spouse. You're much better off to nurture the dating life with your spouse and teach listening skills to him or her.

Same-sex friends can share activities or hobbies or interests that your spouse cannot. For instance, you may be interested in sports and want to talk about the latest play-off games, but your spouse isn't interested.

Debby likes going to dog shows and talking about dogs. She has entered many shows and thinks it's a great hobby. Her husband, Tim, quickly gets bored when the subject turns to bearded collies.

Tim likes playing basketball. Debby likes to shoot around a little on occasion, but she doesn't like playing games.

At first, they tried to participate in each other's interests, but that didn't work. Now they have same-sex friends to do their hobbies with, and both are happy pursuing their own hobbies knowing the other is also having a great time.

When you are with each other, another key to a successful relationship is never to take the other for granted.

Let the Other Person Know How You Feel

A major source of marital dissatisfaction is that spouses feel taken for granted. Much of this has to do with the Thinking/Feeling preference misconceptions (see chapter 5). Telling your spouse something positive, and not the same thing each day, can work wonders.

Tell your partner, "I love you," "You look great," "You're sexy," "I appreciate things you've done to help today," or "I'm glad you married me." These words will be reassuring and very contagious. Before you know it, your partner will start saying appreciative things too.

In the card shops, you see lots of valentine or anniversary cards that say something like, "I know you don't feel appreciated," or "I haven't told you that I love you," or "Sometimes, I can be such a big jerk, but I'm sending you this card to tell you how much I care."

Spouses need to hear how they are loved more than once a year. Every day is best.

Treat Your Spouse As If He or She Is New

One joy of a new relationship is the feeling that your partner adores you. When a couple start dating, each tries hard to please the other. Each spends time finding out what the other likes and then acts on it.

For instance, if a woman's favorite meal is beef Wellington, her infatuated date will go to the store, get all the ingredients, and spend all afternoon preparing it, as well as special drinks, appetizers, and desserts. Of course, his apartment or house will be spotless.

While dating, you go to great lengths to see your loved one. Even if she's hours away, you'll make the trip just so you can be with her for a few hours. Couples who used to make out for hours will share a perfunctory kiss now and then.

Infatuation gives energy. As the relationship matures, the intensity of wanting to please your mate can diminish, but it can be rekindled.

Every now and then treat your spouse like a wonderful new catch. Have a bubble bath waiting; make a favorite meal; go away to a romantic hideaway for the weekend.

Spoil your spouse. And on other occasions, your spouse will spoil you. There is no timetable for how often you should do some major spoiling, but the more the better, at least a few times a year. The pampering shouldn't last only an hour. It's got to be at least an evening, but a whole day is best.

Treating your spouse as if he or she is new will eliminate two of the major causes of marital dissatisfaction: being taken for granted and wanting to feel wanted and vital.

BRINGING LIGHT TO DARKNESS

This chapter looked at Conflict Without Casualty for married couples, preventing problems, and revitalizing relationships. The next chapter looks at the dark side of marriage and how to bring light to it: what to do when things go south, or how to heal your marriage when it's hurting.

What to Do
When Things
Go South

We are all heartened by couples just returning from the honeymoon very much in love and looking forward to a new life together. When conflicts happen—and they are sure to—couples who solve them collaboratively sustain the honeymoon level of joy. People who avoid conflict or try to force their will on to others experience casualty each time there is conflict. This casualty can chip away at their happiness until little delight is left in the relationship. The good news is that by using Conflict Without Casualty techniques, you can sustain happiness and even repair any damage that has been done.

Conflict resolution skills are extremely vital for married couples. Although Conflict Without Casualty is possible for all couples, statistics reveal disturbing data that there is much needless human misery. Half of the couples who giddily open wedding presents will get divorced within a few years. These marriages are cynically known as starter marriages. Statistics aren't collected on how many couples stay married but aren't happy being together, but we have to assume there are many couples who fall into that category. It doesn't have to be that way. For every unhappy couple, there are others who think that getting married was the best thing they ever did. Usually, the happy ones are those who have figured out how to resolve conflicts.

Couples who practice Conflict Without Casualty can develop win-win solutions to problems that would paralyze other couples. Many couples wait until they're in the throes of distress before they learn how to solve their disputes. The solutions are there. Many of my patients tell me that after they learn about personality type and conflict resolution skills, they look at other couples' problems and can't believe they were debilitated by similar ones.

When people use power plays or avoid each other in times of trouble rather than undertake effective relationship-promoting activities, it's like they're dying of thirst, inches from the water fountain. That's a big shame. This chapter surveys what to do and what not to do if a relationship is in trouble. Throwing in the towel is almost always no answer at all. Some of the strategies are effective for married couples; others work only for couples not married yet; and some will work for couples in any phase, dating, engaged, or married.

OUR CULTURE ALLOWS IT

As great as American culture is, we must be mindful of certain aspects of it in regard to relationships. We're exposed to images of how we should act and what we should think many times each day. Although they are not excuses for how we choose to act, these cultural teachings need to be addressed: (1) we take the short view, (2) we're not trained in conflict resolution, (3) marriage is not considered sacred, and (4) divorce is widely accepted as an easy out. Let's look at each and how it affects a relationship.

We Take the Short View

We, as a culture, take the short view. We do it in business and in relationships. Our culture tells us to get rewards as soon as possible. The rewards can be economic, sexual, or emotional. The psychological term for this is *immediate gratification*. Immediate gratification every now and then adds spice to life, but as a life-style, it makes people self-absorbed.

Movies and television programs show couples who meet and have sex soon afterward. Producers defend their actions by saying that is what viewers want to see, and that no one would want to see a movie or program about a couple nurturing and developing a long-term relationship.

A real-life budding relationship doesn't make very good footage, and the sound bites aren't very entertaining. Just ask any waiter or waitress who has a table in "lovers' lane" about how insipid new couples' conversations can be to everyone but them.

"The Love Boat" mentality (a TV show in which week after week a fresh batch of the characters met, fought, made up, and married during a three-day cruise) leaves some viewers feeling bewildered by or inadequate with real-life romances. They feel that something is wrong if they don't instantly fall in love and have terrific sex. Nothing is wrong except that reality can never compete with fiction.

Advertising is another factor that constantly reinforces the need for immediate gratification. You may not realize it, but you see hundreds of ads screaming at you to buy products of all types. The formula is simple: use advertising to make people feel uneasy about their bodies and about their relationships with their family members or with other important people in their lives. Then after their prey are thoroughly disenchanted, the strategy is to give them hope—every problem can be solved quickly and easily by making a purchase.

Madison Avenue spends billions of dollars a year in an attempt to hardwire our brains into believing that problems must be—and can be—solved quickly. And for the vast majority of us, this advertising ploy is successful to varying degrees.

We Want the Quick Fix

We don't like pain and inconvenience. As a society, we want to take pills to solve problems. When we find out that all medicines have side effects of one type or another, we don't want to hear it. We want to have our cake and eat it too.

I get a big kick out of some radio psychologists. People call in their problems, and after listening for a minute or two, the psychologist gives a pat answer that is supposed to "magically" make things better. Hogwash. Problems that take many years to develop won't go away in thirty seconds or even thirty days.

Any long-term relationship has hills and valleys. Some people feel that if they're not happy for a few weeks or a few months, something is wrong with them, their spouses, or their relationships.

Usually, nothing is wrong. They're experiencing a natural cycle. Sometimes people hit the panic button, and they start worrying. All that rumination feeds on itself. This is similar to businesses taking drastic action during economic downturns. Our economy is cyclical, and there will be boom times, lean times, and periods of slow and steady growth. When businesses get into a survival mode and cut inventories, lay off workers, and act as if they're in a permanent downturn, they're panicking.

Businesses that realize that economic slowdowns last a year or so, and treat them with that amount of seriousness, prosper for the long term. Those that overreact often end up out of business.

Feeling sad or bad about yourself or your relationship isn't productive. Talk it through with friends, your minister, or a therapist and, of course, your spouse. While you're working through all that is going on, keep in the back of your mind (1) that this is an expected life event and (2) that it will end. The "bad time" should be treated with a limited amount of worry.

We Forget Why We Got Married in a Church

Before you and your spouse were declared husband and wife, with a solemnness unequaled at any other moment in your life, you made some vows. People get married in a church as a symbol of the covenant they are making with each other and with God.

When you think of it, we don't take many vows in our lives. A vow is a sacred commitment that we make to others that cannot be retracted. Police officers take a vow to protect and to serve; they can't change their minds in the middle of a bank robbery. Physicians take a vow in the Hippocratic oath to put their patients' needs ahead of their own. The president of the United States vows to protect the Constitution.

Most of us make only wedding vows. One might think that all that forsaking others and having to keep someone in bad, poor, and sick times is a prescription for a breakup. That's wrong. Sure, you get some of the above, but you get a whole bunch of good, rich, and healthy times. It's a good trade-off.

When you share your vows, you're forming a covenant. A covenant is the Mount Everest of vows. The good news is that you're not just making a covenant with each other; it's with God and God with you. This covenant is powerful, and you can use its power to your advantage in sustaining a lifelong loving relationship.

At most Christian marriages "those whom God has joined together, let no one put asunder" is proclaimed. Lots of people get so caught up in the moment they can't appreciate the significance of this statement. It brings great strength and comfort to married couples.

The power of God is beyond anything we can fathom. Here are a few examples. God the Father created us and our universe, parted the Red Sea, and knows how many hairs are on our heads. Jesus raised Lazarus from the dead, and He has also taken on the job as Savior of the world. The Holy Spirit creates life and communicates with each of us through the sometimes booming and sometimes still small voice. God has been around for eternity! It would be fair to say that He has had enough experience to give Him a very impressive resume.

It was God's idea that marriage is an ideal place for a man and a woman to live together in love. It takes only until the second chapter of Genesis (vv. 18–24) for Moses to talk about marriage.

Jesus performed His first miracles while attending the wedding in Cana (John 2:1–11). Most Christians see this as an affirmation of marriage. Jesus says that the only out from marriage is in the case of adultery (Matt. 5:31–32). Is that because Jesus wants people to live together in a hostile environment, living less-than-fulfilled lives? Our enemies, not Jesus, want us to be miserable. I don't think that Jesus would have gone through all the trouble of coming to earth and being crucified, cleansing the sin of the world, and resurrecting if it were all so we could be at odds with our spouses.

I'm a big fan of using psychology to help relationships. God invented our brains, and understanding His creation is a positive experience.

You and your spouse got married in a church to seal the covenant that you have with each other and that God has with you. Ask God for help. He is the resource that many people don't rely on.

I can guarantee you that a man and a woman who are married to each other and who want to keep their wedding vows can do it.

They will be happy at the end of the process, even though a great deal of work and heartache may have to happen before they're finished and the work of understanding and appreciating is continued.

Ask God for His help and you'll get it. Don't worry if this is a new revelation. God will be there for you. He has always been there.

Our society can be a difficult one when the going gets tough. Though marriage is a sacred moral commitment, it's an almost meaningless legal one.

Divorce Is Widely Accepted

Marriage as a legal relationship was set up many years ago when women were considered chattel, or property. (In fact, the concept of their not being property in the Western world is only about one hundred years old.) The big concern when there was a divorce was the percentage of the dowry to be paid back, since the woman was no longer a virgin and considered to be "used and damaged goods."

The other important issues were how the assets would be split and how much money the wife would need to support the children.

In most states there is a list of grounds for divorce: adultery, cruel and abusive treatment, neglect, bigamy, and a handful of others. The one used most often is irreconcilable differences that lead to the irremediable breakdown of the marriage.

In most states if you can say the words *irreconcilable differences,* you can get a divorce. The days of fault grounds or one spouse granting a divorce to the other are long gone. Divorcing spouses don't have to prove malfeasance or justify their action. Jilted spouses often beg to know why the terrible action is happening to them. They ask, "What did I do?"

Divorcing spouses never have to answer that question. Divorce is considered to be a right. It's the only legal contract for which there is no penalty for breaking it. Divorce laws are so liberal because at one time spouses murdered their spouses to get out of marriage. Legislators saw so much domestic violence over wanting to end a marriage that they made the process easy. (Psychologists will tell you that many reconcilable marriages end in divorce because divorce is so easy and there is little or no social stigma attached.)

American society doesn't treat marriage as sacred. To many people, the only difference between cohabitation and marriage is a piece of paper and some tax benefits. With so many marriages ending in divorce, officers of the court don't want to hear the gory details. All they want to do is take out their calculators and divide assets. If there are children, callously referred to as "issue," the courts want to do what's best for them—which almost always means giving the mother custody.

In some states men tend to get better settlements; in other states women do. Some people who have made a sacred covenant between themselves and God view the dissolution of the covenant as a simple economic decision. All they can think of is how they'll make out economically.

There is no great stigma in being divorced. It's good that we're forgiving, but it's bad that getting a divorce is so easy.

If couples are getting divorced because they have problems with conflict resolution, that's certainly not a valid reason. They can usually fix the problem. If they don't, they are doomed to repeat the cycle with someone else.

Marriage is a covenant. Yet lots of people slough off marriage vows as words they muttered. Other people say, "I meant them at the time, but I changed my mind." They're missing the whole point of a sacred vow and a covenant—you give up your right to change your mind.

When I start a therapy session with couples, I ask them what their wedding vows were. I use that as a basis for therapy. If they vowed to stay married for better, in health, until they get sick of being married, I might be more sympathetic to their throwing in the towel. Of course, their vows never support the "easy out."

LIFELONG RELATIONSHIPS ARE POSSIBLE

Jesus wants you to stay married to the same person all your life, so the institution can work lifelong. A man and a woman can live together happily and have fulfilled lives with each other. Your job is to figure out how. Your task will be helped if you know that there's a solution, and when you find it, it's worth it.

Later, we'll review some common problems and some solutions. But first, we'll look at the pluses and minuses of common sources of advice.

SOURCES OF ADVICE

When couples have problems with their marriages, the most common sources of advice are friends, therapists, clergypersons, and lawyers.

Friends

For thousands of years, friends were the most common form of support for people in psychological need. Friends know you very well, don't charge you eighty dollars an hour, and often use sophisticated psychological techniques without knowing it.

Women get together with other women and men with other men, and they talk about frustrations and temptations and have an informal support group.

Dave is a twenty-four-year-old newlywed. He and his wife, Theresa, conceived their first child after being married for only a month. They didn't have sex until their wedding day, and Dave was looking forward to spending lots of time making love with Theresa. In the last few months of her pregnancy, sex was difficult and infrequent. After the baby was born, she spent necessary time with the baby. Sometimes he and Theresa would be in the middle of making love and the baby would start crying and her mother hormones would win out over her wife hormones, and that would be the end of that.

Dave had lots of pent-up sexual energy and was feeling tired, frustrated, and not at all happy with his marriage. He talked to his friend, Dean, who had three kids, about his feelings. Dean told Dave, "What's happening to you has happened to every guy since Adam. A couple of months after the baby was born I made plans to go away someplace nice alone with my wife for a long weekend. Also, spend lots of couple time while the baby is sleeping."

Dean owns and manages three parking garages, but his advice is worthy of any licensed psychologist.

Some friends have a little psychological knowledge and know just enough to be dangerous. Other people have had therapy and think that qualifies them to make diagnoses and recommend treatments. They give advice that is hurtful.

Lynn took abnormal psychology courses in college and has been seeing a therapist for a couple of years. When her friend Marla asked for advice about her fiancé, Bob, and why he took so many business trips, Lynn told her that he was using his job as a vehicle for denying that he had a fear of commitment.

Marla asked her fiancé about that, and he told her that he just had more than average travel because his business had announced a new product.

Lynn told Marla that it was classic denial behavior and that Bob was projecting his fears onto his job. Lynn further suggested to Marla that she postpone the wedding until he dealt with his problems or else she was doomed to a codependent relationship.

Marla did. She ended up not getting married.

"See," Lynn told her, "he had a fear of commitment or else he wouldn't have called things off."

In this example, Marla's fiancé didn't have a fear of commitment, but he did have an extraordinarily heavy travel schedule. He resented being accused of a fear of commitment, and he was embarrassed to tell all of his friends that his marriage was being postponed because he took five two-day business trips.

Diagnosis is complex. It takes years of training and practice. Interpersonal problems can be quite involved. A good rule of thumb is that most behavior means nothing. Doctors are taught in medical school that if they hear hoofs galloping to look for horses and not for zebras. That means look at the most obvious reason for a behavior first and then go to the more complex. If someone walks into a doctor's office with a cough, the doctor will first assume that the patient has a cold and not immediately start testing for malaria.

If Lynn had psychological training, she would have known that when Marla's fiancé said that his travel schedule was heavy and temporary, it meant nothing more than that.

Another trait of friends is that they may not speak negatively about your loved one.

> Sam dated Judy for three years. All of Sam's friends told him how much they liked her. After Sam and Judy broke up, they all started telling him how much they disliked her. Some thought she was a difficult and demanding person. Others said that all she did was complain.
>
> After Judy, Sam knew that no matter how much people said they liked who he was dating, it didn't matter; they could think of her as little as they thought of Judy.

Friends can be a source of comfort and commonsense advice. But you have to make sure that the advice they give you is moral and consistent with your values.

Therapists

Therapists can have many different titles—psychotherapist, psychiatrist, counselor, etc. None of the titles necessarily will tell you whether someone is qualified and competent, however. Here is what to watch out for.

You would hope that people who get into helping professions do so for altruistic reasons. The responsibility I feel for my patients is incredible. (By the way, I call the people who see me patients, not because they are sick, but because they are hurting and have placed their trust in me and my skill. When I do corporate conflict resolution, I call the people who see me clients because they are not entrusting their lives and happiness with me.)

Unfortunately, many therapists get into the business because (1) they like learning personal secrets about other people and (2) they have problems of their own that they try to solve through their patients and clients. If you suspect your therapist is in either category, find someone else. I've identified some specific red flags.

Red Flag 1: You See the Therapist Alone

When having relationship problems, a couple must solve them together. Alone, a spouse can present an unrealistic picture of the other spouse. Over 90 percent of the time when people see therapists alone, they end up breaking up with the mate.

Red Flag 2: Marriage and Dating are Viewed Similarly

Many therapists regard dating, engaged, and married couples as the same, and they make the same recommendations for all three types. There is folly in that logic. A trend in the nineties is to place an inordinate emphasis on personal growth. This type of therapist also thinks that personal growth can take place only outside the boundaries of marriage. That's flat out wrong.

Therapists know that seeing someone alone is virtually a ticket to a breakup. Still, they strive to "empower" their clients to "find themselves." They get a thrill when the people who come to see them do things they themselves never could. They see themselves in their clients. It's part of what is technically called *countertransference*. It's wrong, ethically and morally.

I had a conversation with an ethics professor at a major New England college. She held the theory that all familial and relationship problems are created by men subjugating and manipulating women, which is a very popular position on many college campuses. There are men who are horrible to women, and there are women who are horrible to men. People are far too complex to clump into two piles and expect all members of each sex to act the same way.

This professor described the case of a forty-year-old woman with three children and a fifteen-year-old marriage who was complaining of being stifled. The woman moved directly from her parents' house to her husband's, and she had never been on her own. This therapist thought the only intervention (treatment) was to recommend divorce or separation so the client could become her own woman and "find herself."

I told her that would be unconscionable. The patient's need for self-growth could be achieved in the marriage, and even if one problem would be solved, another would be created. A person is more empowered with the knowledge to solve a problem rather than flee it.

Many therapists feel important because they can wheedle people into leaving the spouse. Once the divorce is over, they feel that their mission is accomplished, and they cut their clients loose. Many are left with regrets like Deidre, a forty-five-year-old mother of four:

> After I left my husband, Hal, he was devastated. My children hated me because they had to move and they could see their father only once a week. Now I feel so all alone. Hal is dating a thirty-five-year-old accountant who is gorgeous, and I'm finding that my dating life is nonexistent. I never should have left. If this is growth, I think it stinks. To make matters worse my therapist told me I've grown so much that I don't need to see her anymore.

The bottom line is that if you want to see a therapist, see that person with your spouse. The odds for reconciliation go way up— about a 90 percent chance of success. Some people are reluctant to broach the subject of therapy with the spouse. But almost universally, spouses are willing to go along, especially when they know the danger involved in one spouse's going alone. (Show your spouse this part of the book if necessary.) You want to say something like this to your mate:

> I love you so much. I want to see a therapist because I'm not as happy as I would like to be. The problem is that I know that if I see a therapist, the person is going to talk about you as the problem. Also, the odds of something terrible happening are too much for me. Will you go and help me work on this concern?

Red Flag 3: Your Therapist Recommends a Trial Separation

If a therapist recommends a trial separation, run, don't walk, away from that therapist (except in the case of spousal abuse). About 95 percent of trial separations end in final separations.

Think of how many couples you know who had a trial separation that eventually ended their relationship. Most.

The theory is that while the couple are separated, absence will make the heart grow fonder. Some couples even have elaborate contracts drawn up that prohibit dating and delineate behaviors that can and cannot go on. The theory is flawed. If communication is a problem, the way to solve the problem is not less communication.

If you are separated now, contact your spouse and suggest working out your problems together. You can give as a reason that the odds are heavily stacked against you if you remain separated.

Red Flag 4: Your Therapist Wants to Date or Have Sex with You

Because of your special relationship with your therapist, you are ripe pickings for someone looking to take advantage of the situation. Therapist-patient sex is generally with a male therapist and a female patient, but the reverse is also true. This phenomenon happens because patients psychologically see their therapist as someone else in their lives, called *transference*.

If you're thinking that having sex with someone who really understands you and you trust explicitly isn't such a bad thing, think again. You're playing with forces that are evil and usually beyond your control. That relationship is destined to hurt you. That's why the American Psychological Association and every other psychological association ban such behavior. Sometimes therapists are prohibited from dating a patient for two years after counseling ends, but usually, dating is never permitted.

If at any time your therapist suggests having a dating or sexual relationship, leave immediately and report that person to your state's attorney general.

A Therapist Can Help

A therapist can help you and your mate if you're not happy or not as happy as you could be. A good therapist has often seen the types of problems that you and your mate are having. The therapist knows what works and what doesn't. Also, an ethical therapist will do all that he or she can to help you keep your marriage vows.

Some therapists follow a certain psychological model. Others mix approaches and take ideas from several theories. I find that when therapists try to pigeonhole patients into their particular model, some patients lose out.

Still, the therapist can clarify issues, see patterns, recommend changes, and provide support during difficult times. You're paying for someone's knowledge and expertise, just like you would pay for an accountant's expertise. You're not paying for a friend.

You may have problems that create other problems, and perhaps the way you and your spouse deal with each other causes resentments. Discovering the patterns takes skill, and it takes tenacity by the therapist and the patients.

As useful as therapists are, some people think that turning to a therapist for help is taking the easy way out. Anyone who has been to therapy knows that therapy can be fascinating, but it is work.

God gave us physicians and others for a reason: to help us and to heal us. Let me share with you a passage that speaks to this issue from Ecclesiasticus, one of the books in the Apocrypha:

> Honor the physician with the honor due him, according to your need of him, for the Lord has created him, for the healing comes from the Most High, and he will receive a gift from the King. The skill of the physician lifts up his head, and in the presence of great men he is admired. The Lord created medicines from the earth, and a sensible man will not despise them. . . . And he gave skill to men that he might be glorified in his marvelous works. By them he heals and takes away pain; the pharmacist makes of them a compound. His works will never be finished; and from him health is upon the face of the earth. My son, when you are sick do not be negligent, but pray to the Lord, and he will heal you. Give up your faults and direct your hands upright, and cleanse your heart from all sin. . . . And give the physician his place, for the Lord created him; let him not leave you, for there is need of him. There is a time when success lies in the hands of physicians, for they too will pray to the Lord that he should grant them success in

diagnosis and in healing, for the sake of preserving life (Ecclus. 38:1-4, 6-10, 12-14 RSV).

Finding a Therapist

Finding a suitable therapist takes some effort, and most people don't know where to start. A few pointers will make your job easier. If you're Christian, I strongly recommend a Christian therapist. If you are not Christian, I recommend a therapist who values the sanctity of marriage as a covenant.

The first step should be to speak to your priest or minister. Get at least two or three names and call them up. Promising results is grounds for malpractice, so therapists won't give you guarantees. Here are some questions to ask:

- What is your theoretical background, if any?
- Do you recommend trial separations?
- Do you see the spouses together? Or do you prefer to see a spouse alone?
- What are your fees?
- What is the average time that people see you?
- What is your success rate in preserving marriage?
- What is your religious affiliation?

Some therapists have a theoretical background (a type of therapy that they prefer). There are no absolutes about any type of therapy being better than any other type. But some therapies are more effective with some people and some problems.

You may be the type who likes to work things out on your own. For you, a Rogerian psychologist, who feels you have the answers to your problems but need assistance in finding them, would be best. Others like a more direct approach, which is what I use.

Another good source of advice is pastors. Let's take a look at them.

Pastors

Pastors spend a good amount of time counseling church members as well as people not in their church. It seems as if pastors have dealt with every situation under the sun. Don't worry that a particular set of circumstances or life event may be judged harshly by them—pastors are there to provide help and spiritual direction and forgiveness.

The most positive aspect of pastoral counseling is that a pastor will respect your marriage vows and will not—like some therapists—recommend dissolution of the marriage as the quick fix to every problem.

Also, a pastor will provide direction that is consistent with your faith. I'm a strong believer that emotional healing is easiest and more complete when it's done in tandem with a person's faith.

Finally, pastoral counseling is often free or low cost.

There are some traps. First, some states limit the number of visits one can get counseling from a clergyperson because of licensing requirements (unless the visit is purely for spiritual direction). Many pastors fear being sued for malpractice, and in some locales any visit after six is fair game for lawyers.

Also, some pastors have specific education and training in counseling, while others do not. The one or two courses they took in seminary can make them know just enough to be dangerous. If this is the case, use a therapist and a pastor together to provide for all of your needs.

Let's look at another form of advice, lawyers.

Lawyers

Lawyers will give you legal opinions. The American Bar Association's ethical code dictates that a lawyer has a responsibility to do all he or she can to keep a couple together. Some abide by the ethical code, but others give it lip service, or ignore the code altogether.

And why not? Breaking you and your spouse up will net them $3,000 to $10,000. They may bash your spouse and make promises of riches if you separate. There's an old adage: In a divorce divide what you have into quarters; you and your spouse get a quarter and the lawyers get half!

Be very careful about the advice lawyers give. Although they are supposed to have your best interests in mind, they often do not. Here is the exception:

If you are in an abusive relationship and you fear for your life or well-being, a lawyer can be of great assistance. The attorney can get a temporary restraining order, find you a shelter, and keep you safe. They know the system and will use every legal method they can to make sure that their clients do not become a sad statistic (see the appendix).

Now, let's look at some of the issues that can sour a relationship.

TIME TOGETHER

Couples need to spend time together. However, we all have a different need for togetherness. When both members of the couple want to be with each other the same amount, that works out well. But when there is a disparity, trouble begins.

Jane likes being with her husband, Murray. However, Murray has recently developed a friendship with some buddies, and they like going to a neighbor's rec room and playing pool. At first, Jane didn't mind the once-a-week game, but six months later it's three or four times a week.

She doesn't like being alone at night. She is starting to think that if Murray doesn't want to spend time with her, she might as well leave him.

Ironically, many people think that the solution to wanting to see the spouse more is to leave the spouse. When you look into this more deeply, you'll see that people like Jane don't like being alone. That's not a character flaw; that's a trait. Wanting to be with people is as much a trait as having blue eyes.

A couple works out the issue of how much time to be with each other early in the dating process.

Zach has dated Cathy each Friday night for the past two weeks. He is very attracted to her and wants to date her more. He typically spends five or six nights a week with a current girlfriend. Cathy works as an accountant and goes out only once or twice a week. After the second date in five nights, they never saw each other again. Cathy got tired of the barrage of invitations, and Zach got tired of being turned down.

This very important issue cannot be discarded. Many couples find a good balance when they're first dating, but as they date longer or get married, the patterns change. If this happens, here's what to do.

Couples need to spend time together doing enjoyable activities. You'd think that if one member of a couple was unhappy, both members would know. Most often one spouse doesn't realize there's a problem, while the other spouse is in torment. Let's go back to the example of Jane and Murray.

> When Murray was asked about what was going on in his marriage, he didn't understand. He didn't know that Jane was unhappy. He said that he couldn't for the life of him figure out why she was upset. I asked him if he had any ideas, and he said no. I asked him if he thought that he and Jane weren't spending a lot of time together. He said yes, but it was her choice.
>
> "My choice," Jane responded. "I can't believe you're saying that."
>
> "What do you mean? I ask you if you want to go out with me every night, and you always say no. I wish you would come out with me."
>
> "You know I don't want to go out and watch you shoot pool with lots of guys swearing, drinking, and talking about sports."
>
> "I didn't know you were so upset. What can we do about it?"

The "what they can do about it" will take a while for them to work out, but at least both know that there is a problem. What happened to Jane and Murray is a classic case of couples who are communicating but not talking the same language. Jane needs to learn that she can't wait a year to voice her concerns for two reasons. First, she'll be needlessly unhappy. Second, it's much easier to solve one problem at a time rather than wait and solve the entire year's problems in one fell swoop.

Therapists are accustomed to seeing the pent-up frustrations that people have been keeping inside them for a long time.

You Can Eat an Elephant

Sometimes someone is so disenchanted that resolving all of the issues seems an insurmountable task. It's almost like the problems are an elephant that the couple have to eat in one sitting.

You can eat an elephant, but only one bite at a time. When I see couples, I ask them to tell me the biggest problems; then I show them the collaborative problem-solving method. In the first session, we usually solve one or two major problems. Then as they learn the technique, they solve more and more problems collaboratively on their own. You have to start chipping away, and you'll find that all of your concerns and all of your mate's concerns will be met—but not in one afternoon.

MONEY PROBLEMS

Many couples have money problems. Before I get into more specifics, I think it's appropriate to explain why I am including financial information in this book. Millions of couples divorce each year or needlessly suffer through a hurtful time in their marriages because they are having financial problems that can be solved. Through their business practices, banks, credit card companies, and anyone else that extends credit may contribute to breaking the covenant between you, your spouse, and God. And they can be very devious. Your marriage vows are more important than any financial commitment you will ever make, and that's why it's critical that you are armed to the teeth with accurate information.

There Are Many Types

Money problems take many shapes. Sometimes it's because there's too much debt, and other times it's because there's not enough income. Couples find themselves in these circumstances because of job loss, medical bills, or other unplanned expenses, such as major house repairs.

Other times couples make large amounts of charge purchases and then find themselves not being able to pay the bills. It's very common, especially for newlyweds, to get suckered into making lots of purchases on credit.

When credit is given out, creditors make it seem so easy, with promises of low monthly payments. MasterCard, Visa, Discover, and American Express spend tens of millions of dollars a year convincing us that credit cards are "smart money." What they don't tell you is that if you only pay the minimum monthly payments at 18 percent interest, it can be decades before you pay off the balance.

Other times, because of job loss, or some other emergency, couples have to take out loans to make mortgage and other payments. Before they know it, they're in hock up to their eyeballs.

The point is that even the most careful of people can get into trouble. The best of all possible worlds is that money problems never happen. Prevention is certainly the best medicine. Before getting into what couples need to do if they are having money difficulties, let's go over some basic advice from financial counselors.

Using Credit

What are effective and ineffective uses of credit and how can people tell if they're getting in too deep? Here are some good uses for credit:

1. To buy a home. Buying a home is usually a sound investment to get tax benefits and appreciation. Many financial advisors will say that the worst invention ever is the home equity credit line. This is because the equity couples have in their home is a great safety net. Since it's possible to borrow almost all of the equity in a home, when unexpected problems hit a couple, they have no recourse. Also, if people use their home as collateral, if they cannot pay the debt secured by the home, they will lose the place they live.

(Although it's not pleasant to sell a home and use the proceeds to pay bills, getting a mortgage on another home will usually not be difficult.)

2. To buy a car. Cars are expensive and many people need one to get to work. If you have to get a loan to buy a car, status should not be a prime consideration. Obtain the cheapest car you can that you consider reliable and safe. Financial advisors say that a two-year loan is best and to never have a loan longer than three years. (Though a five-year loan offers lower payments, the car may not last that long. The sooner you own your car, the sooner it will be an asset and not a liability.)

3. Education. The payback on education makes it one of the best investments you can get. Rules have loosened in the past few years, and many people can now qualify for low-interest government-backed loans.

That's it for effective uses of credit. Here are some ways people use credit that are not effective:

1. Any non-asset purchase. A good example of a non-asset purchase is a vacation: When you are back from it, you don't have anything tangible. It's common for couples to charge their wedding reception, engagement and wedding rings, and their honeymoon and after it's all over have a mountain of debt to deal with. The best present a couple can give to each other is financial security.

2. Consumer items. Consumer items (such as VCRs, CD players, boats) are not good to take loans out for unless the payments for those items are less than 2 percent of monthly take-home income.

3. Restaurants, gas, and food. You can use your credit card at a restaurant, to buy gas, and even at the supermarket. Unless this is absolutely necessary, avoid these practices since you can run up huge bills and have nothing as an asset except the memories. Also, credit card companies know we are much more likely to spend additional money at restaurants if we don't pay cash.

How do people know if they're getting in too deep? These are not hard-and-fast rules, but here are some warning signs that money problems are getting serious:

- You are not sure how much you owe.
- Your monthly installment payments (not mortgage) are more than 20 percent of income.
- You skip some payments to some creditors in order to pay others, or you let all payments run late.
- You need to take out a loan to pay another loan.
- You need to extend repayment times.
- You cannot meet emergencies.

- You borrow large amounts of money from family or friends.
- You gamble to try to make the quick strike and pay everything off. (This never works and makes matters worse.)
- You borrow money from a loan shark.
- You find yourself lying on tax returns to get a bigger refund. (The IRS will eventually catch you on this, and you will have more problems than you can possibly imagine.)

Also, be aware of the following behavioral changes.

- You are losing sleep.
- You are arguing with your spouse and family over little issues.
- Money seems to be an all-consuming worry.
- You cannot talk about financial matters with your spouse without an argument.

A Full Till

If a couple has to struggle to make ends meet, there's not much to argue about—all the money has to go to pay for necessities. Ironically, when a couple gets more money, there's a surplus, and that's when lots of arguing may begin. One spouse wants to buy a pool, while the other wants to go to Paris or send the kids to private school. It may seem that too much money is a good problem, and it can be. But many times, too much money just brings a different set of problems.

This type of conflict is like any other. Couples need to address concerns and come to a collaborative solution.

Probably a more common type of problem is too little money. Now let's take a look at that.

An Empty Till

Money problems can adversely affect a relationship. Bill collectors get a percentage of what they collect, so they relentlessly dog you to get their commission. Collectors hope to position you in the yield-lose mode and hope to gain advantage by your wanting to avoid a confrontation with them. In many cases they know the laws and you don't. Of course, they use that to their advantage. The reality is that you have your rights and options too.

Here is how most collections calls go:

> *Collector:* I see that you owe $2,000 on your MasterCard, and you haven't made a payment in several months. When can we expect a payment?
>
> *Beth:* I'm sorry I'm behind, but I [got laid off, had a baby, had emergency medical expenses, my car broke down, etc.].
>
> *Collector:* If I don't receive $200 by the end of the month, I'm going to report this to the credit bureau.
>
> *Beth:* I'll pay. I'll pay.

When Beth's husband comes home, she tells him what the collector said and tells him that they have to come up with $200 by month's end. Their situation has gone from bad to worse.

> *John:* Two hundred dollars! Why did you promise an idiotic thing like that? How are we going to come up with that much money? You should have called me at work. You know that I have this other job that I have to pay these stupid bills.
>
> *Beth:* I'm sorry. I'm working as hard as I can, too, you know.
>
> *John:* That does us a lot of good.

Beth is angry with herself for caving in to the collector. John is angry with himself because he doesn't want to make the payment. Unfortunately, the bill collector isn't at their house to yell at. If he were, they'd give him a piece of their minds, but since he is not, they yell at each other instead. Even though they're just blowing off steam, it's not a very pleasant scene. New computerized telephone systems are relentless and will hound you until you feel like a prisoner in your own home.

Don't feel badly if you're at odds with your creditors. They are very good at trying to wear you down.

Bill collectors hope that they can divide the couple and create disharmony. The rationale is that if you and your mate constantly fight over bills, you will try to end the harassment and the disharmony by paying them. They know that you and your spouse are a formidable team when you are acting together so they try to split you.

The power of your commitment and your love for each other, as well as the laws set to protect you (I'll talk about them below), are no match. You can work your way out of this dilemma.

Realities of Being in Debt

The usury laws, or the laws that regulate how much businesses can charge for interest, have changed a lot in the last twenty years. Not that long ago, people got thrown in jail for charging 18 percent interest because that was the rate only Louis the Loan Shark charged. Now major banks charge that rate—and even higher.

Banks and credit card companies previously required you to pay lots of principal and a little interest each month. The monthly payments were high enough to pay off the card in two years. That was a check and balance. Most credit card companies had a formula for acceptance based on the total amount of your current monthly payments, so with high monthly payments you'd only be able to get one or two cards.

Today, you're paying mostly interest and a little principal. If you have a used-up two-thousand-dollar credit limit and are making only minimum monthly payments, it can take you thirty to fifty years to pay off that credit card. What if you have ten credit cards and all your extra money is going for the minimum payments, which are made up mostly of interest? You got it. Paying off the cards can take forty or fifty years; you're working for those companies.

How Banks Work

Banks get money in many ways, but the two most common ones are having deposit accounts and buying money from the federal government. They buy it from the government at the discount rate, which is about half the maximum they pay on savings accounts. Banks pay interest on checking and savings accounts from 2 to 6 percent.

Banks borrow money cheaply, much more cheaply than you or I can. The government wants banks to make profits, so it loans them money at 3 percent and allows them to loan it to you at 18 to 24 percent. What a deal! But it gets better—for the banks, not for you.

If the bank goes bankrupt, which happens hundreds of times a year and costs billions of dollars, who pays for the bankruptcy? We do. The Federal Deposit Insurance Corporation (FDIC) will bail out failed banks by paying all their bills, including deposits, usually up to one hundred thousand dollars per account. One reason our taxes have gone up recently is all the billions and billions of dollars that we, the taxpayers, have had to shell out because of bad decisions made by banks.

Finding Solutions

When those harassing phone calls from bill collectors come in, they forget to mention that you have some options that will end your financial problems. Too many marriages needlessly suffer while large companies with huge assets snicker as they profit at the expense of their customers.

First of all, every state is different in offering protection from creditors. See an attorney to find out how information in this chapter can benefit you. The attorney knows that if you have financial problems, you don't have truckloads of cash, and he or she will work out a payment plan that won't break you further. Most attorneys provide a free initial consultation. Talk to the attorney about that beforehand so you won't have any surprises.

Basically, you have two options to confront and solve your problems.

Option 1: The CCCS

Your first option is the Consumer Credit Counseling Service (CCCS). This nonprofit company is financed by major banks and credit card companies. You can call the CCCS toll-free at 1-800-388-2227. The CCCS will charge you a one-time fee of ten dollars and will even waive that fee if it would strap you too much.

The company will negotiate with all of your creditors, and all of your dealings with the CCCS are confidential. First, the counselors will get details of your budget and income. Then they'll make a financial plan that works for you. If your problem is too much interest, they'll negotiate with the banks to lower or eliminate the interest. They may lower the debt or the monthly payments too. This solution is good for the banks because they'll get their principal back (they wouldn't if you went bankrupt), although at a lower interest rate and it may take longer.

You get interest relief and payments that you can afford. You also get harassment relief. When you make a deal, your creditors will be prohibited from contacting you as long as you keep your end of the bargain. Often the payment plan with the CCCS will be on your credit report. Some future creditors may look at this as a negative because you weren't able to meet the original terms of the obligations. Others will look at it as a positive because you are working to pay back as much as you can.

The CCCS helps many people and can be just what the credit card doctor ordered. Here is the experience of John and Denise:

John and Denise put a lot of their wedding, honeymoon, and furniture expenses on several credit cards. Their total debt on the cards is $20,000. They made the monthly payments until John's car was stolen right after he had his paycheck cashed with all the money in the glove compartment.

They are two months behind in bills. They got the "everybody forgets sometimes" reminder, the "your account is overdue" notice, and the "your credit privileges are frozen" warning. They just received the "we're going to take legal action" threat.

Both John and Denise are losing sleep and are on edge. They argue about little things too much and are miserable. They called the CCCS and set up an appointment.

Here is their situation:

Total Debt	Monthly Payments	Principal Paid	Interest Rate	Years to Pay Off
$20,000	$350	$34	19%	49

This means at the end of the first month, after paying $350, they pay off only $34 on the total debt. Starting the second month, they owe $19,966, practically the same amount.

They're staring at making these payments for the rest of their lives. To make matters worse, when they run into financial problems, the banks turn on them.

The CCCS negotiated a break on the interest they have already paid, bringing the principal down to $16,000. Next, interest on future payments would be eliminated if they would keep to their payment schedule. Finally, the payments were reduced to $200 per month, which they could afford. Here is what was left:

Total Debt	Monthly Payments	Principal Paid	Interest Rate	Years to Pay Off
$16,000	$200	$200	0%	6½

They now have monthly payments they can afford, get to keep their furniture, and have high hopes that the end is near.

Denise said that the CCCS was a godsend and that her and John's relationship is better than ever.

Not everyone's experience with the CCCS is so rosy, however.

Elaine and Calvin had $40,000 in consumer debt, and Elaine was five months pregnant. Elaine wanted to work half-time in her job but couldn't do so with the heavy monthly payments that they were making. When she and Calvin went to the CCCS, the counselors told them that they had the money to make the payments. They said, "We do now, but not after the baby is born." The counselors told them they wouldn't make an adjustment because they felt that under the circumstances Elaine should be working and not taking care of their baby.

Elaine was crushed. She said that she didn't want to miss her baby's growing up.

After meeting with the CCCS counselors, Elaine and Calvin had to look at other options. They considered filing for bankruptcy.

210 The Fight-Free Marriage

Option 2: Bankruptcy[1]

If you ask most people about bankruptcy, they will tell you that you lose all of your assets, your savings, and your retirement fund; you won't get credit for many years; and you have to go through the public humiliation of facing a judge and jury and a courtroom full of judgmental peers. Most of this information is incorrect or partially true.

First of all, there is no public humiliation in going bankrupt. The vast majority of people never see a judge. You fill out a form that lists creditors and assets. A court-appointed trustee, usually a lawyer experienced in this form of law, will meet with you and your lawyer. The meeting is called a first meeting of creditors, but your creditors know that your debt to them will most likely be discharged, so they usually don't show up. (Usually credit card companies show up when they have knowledge that the debtor has large sums of money squirreled away.)

As soon as you inform your creditors that you have filed for bankruptcy, they almost always choose to write off your debt, and that's that. If you tell them to contact your attorney, they are prohibited by federal law from contacting you ever again.

There are two types of personal bankruptcy, Chapter 11 and Chapter 7. Chapter 11 is very similar to the type of arrangement that you would have with the CCCS, except that it's binding for you and the credit card companies.

In Chapter 11, you keep many of your assets, and the court determines an amount that you can afford to pay. You pay it to the court, which disburses the funds to your creditors. The court decides how long you will make these payments, but it's usually several years. (Some debts can't be discharged—your attorney will let you know which ones.)

Chapter 7 bankruptcy is the discharge of all of your debts. The amount of your assets that you can keep varies from state to state, so ask your lawyer what the figures are for where you live. Because of the Employee Retirement Income Security Act (ERISA), qualified pension plans and many employee stock plans are sacred cows that you can keep no matter how much is in them—even a half million dollars.

Each state lets you keep some assets: cars to a certain value, some equity in your house (known as the homestead exemption), furniture, clothing, kitchen stuff up to a certain amount, and a host of other assets—usually at their depreciated value. If you bought a car or other secured purchases on credit, you may lose them. Fill out the forms with complete candor and honesty, and you'll be all right. If you fudge, even a little bit, it will come back to haunt you.

Bankruptcy can be straightforward or much more complicated. Your attorney will let you know your situation.

Here are common questions about bankruptcy:

Question: Will I ever get credit again?

Answer: You can go bankrupt only once every seven years.

Advice: Most bankruptcy attorneys strongly advise their clients against getting consumer credit after they've gone bankrupt and certainly not for at least eighteen months afterward. Learn new spending patterns before you get into trouble again.

Question: What will people say?

Answer: There are hundreds of thousands of bankruptcy applications each year. It's not the type of thing that people talk about, but with that number each year, you probably know someone who has been through it. You never can control what people will think or say. It's important, though, that you face your financial problems and take appropriate action that will solve them—and protect your marriage.

Question: Should I get a lawyer?

Answer: Yes. The information in this chapter is intended to be general information on bankruptcy and is not intended to be a substitute for an attorney. Remember, bankruptcy lawyers know you're in financial trouble and will figure out a way for you to pay them.

You can file bankruptcy by filling out the forms on your own and paying the filing fee and submitting your case at federal court. But I *strongly* advise you to seek counsel if you decide to choose bankruptcy as your way out of a financial mess. There are several reasons. First, by law, creditors can no longer contact you; they have to call your lawyer. This can take an incredible amount of stress off you and your spouse. Second, all the people involved in the bankruptcy process (your creditors, the trustee, etc.) work with this every day. For you, it is likely to be a once-in-a-lifetime event. An attorney will make sure that you aren't intimidated by the system. Third, the laws are different from state to state and change regularly. An attorney will know all of them and advise you on making the best decisions for you and your family.

Question: Is bankruptcy moral?

Answer: This is a "gray area" moral/ethical decision. The concept of bankruptcy has been around in one form or another for centuries. (For example, in the Old Testament book of Leviticus, creditors were required to forgive debt every seven years.) And just because you go bankrupt, there's no prohibition against paying people back after it's over. If you decide to do this, you can pay off creditors on your terms when you can afford to.

Your relationship with your spouse is a sacred bond. Although your relationship with creditors is not to be taken lightly, it's nothing more than a business contract. Although you will want to work hard to fulfill your obligations and promises in all relationships, *protect your marriage ahead of the interest of the banks.*

You also have the CCCS and Chapter 11 as full payback strategies if you decide, for any reason, that you want to go with them.

Money is a big source of misunderstanding and conflict in marriage. Another dimension, especially for engaged couples, is religion.

The best case is that couples never have problems, and if you find yourself having problems cut the use of credit and seek help. Sometimes you can call creditors and make arrangements with them directly. Other times you can have organizations such as the CCCS go to bat for you. Finally, if nothing else works, and you have no other options, talk to an attorney about your most drastic remedy, Chapter 7 or Chapter 11 bankruptcy.

RELIGION

Faith is an integral part of life. Spiritual teachings are ingrained in us from a very early age. We had no choice in the church we attended when we were young; we went where our parents went.

If our parents were Episcopalian, we went to the Episcopal church. If Catholicism was more appropriate for us, there was no way we would go to that church until we were much older.

Before tackling the subject of interfaith marriages, let's look at marriages where both parties are Christian but of different denominations or no denomination at all.

At first blush this doesn't seem like such a big problem. Both spouses are Christian and hold Christian values.

To some it's not a big deal, but to others it's a huge problem. People can hold dearly certain aspects of their faith that are not present in other flavors of Christianity. For instance, an essential aspect of Catholicism is transubstantiation, or the sacrament of the Eucharist, in which the priest blesses bread and makes it literally into the body of Jesus. Also, the wine the priest blesses becomes literally the blood of Jesus.

Protestant denominations, with the exception of Lutherans, believe the Eucharist is a sacred symbol of Jesus' body and blood, and not the actual body and blood.

This is more than semantics; it makes a basic difference in how people view a sacrament and how they view the importance of the sacrament.

Christians differ on many issues: birth control, specifically how sin is reconciled, who gets into heaven and how, what heaven is like, original sin, and everything to do with the Bible (its meaning, who wrote it, which books to be included, and the meaning of virtually every passage).

When you think about it, Christians agree on precious few issues: Jesus as Lord and Savior, the resurrection of Jesus, and the existence and nature of the Trinity. All Christians agree on the importance of baptism in some form, Eucharist in some form, and ministry in some form.[2] The form is left for each Christian to decide.

There have been arguments about which denomination is best since the early church. Paul, in his first letter to the Corinthians, talks about people wanting to follow his teaching or that of Apollos or Cephas: "Now I say this, that each of you says, 'I am of Paul,' or 'I am of Apollos,' or 'I am of Cephas,' or 'I am of Christ.' Is Christ divided? Was Paul crucified for you? Or were you baptized in the name of Paul?" (1 Cor. 1:12–13).

Today, we could replace Paul, Apollos, or Cephas with the denominations, and it would be just as appropriate. Even nondenominational churches hold to biblical interpretations and worship whose forms are at least as organized as those of denominations.

Similar Personality Types

After doing many personality workshops in churches, something interesting I have discovered is that many of the people who attend a particular church have a similar personality type.

For instance, ESTJs in their daily lives like knowing what the rules are and then keeping them. It makes sense that they would gravitate toward churches that have much structure in their faith and list do's and don'ts.

INFPs like thinking about theories, and they like harmony. They want everyone to be happy and feel good about going to church. Therefore, they gravitate toward churches that focus on the big picture and stress loving God and loving your neighbor as the cornerstone of the Christian faith (Matt: 22:37–40). INFPs like churches that emphasize the Gospels.

No way is better or worse, but both ways are different. If the INFP Christian and the ESTJ Christian were to discuss their faith, they would express very different ideas.

I think that diversity is a good idea in Christianity because with a variety of denominations there is a place for everyone. People of all personality types can find a church or denomination that fits them and allows them to serve God to their full potential. Larger churches such as the Catholic church have diversity at the parish level. For instance, a parish on one side of town may hold traditional values and have very staid church services, while on the other side of town, another Catholic parish may be modern and hold energetic services.

Faith As a Wedge

Diversity in Christian thought can act like a wedge, driving some couples apart. That is in large part because messages about faith have been instilled in us since birth. With that kind of indoctrination, we tend to look at the situation dispassionately.

However, diversity of thought, like a hybrid crop, can yield a stronger output. Two people can learn from each other instead of avoiding theological discussions. A fruitful approach is to explain what you believe and why you believe it without trying to convert your spouse to your viewpoint. Also, listen and be open to understanding your spouse's perspective.

Jesus' ministry was one of love, and it makes sense that He does not want couples who love each other to break up over different styles of worshiping Him.

If you and your mate are both Christian but of different denominations, try the following approach.

Learn as Much as You Can About the Other's Beliefs

Learn about the beliefs from a knowledgeable source that holds the beliefs. Protestants or nondenominational Christians write books about Catholicism and vice versa. The most frequent technique is building a straw man (making statements or assertions that do not accurately reflect the true thought of what is being written about).

For example, a common misconception among non-Catholics is that Catholics pray to statues. Wrong. They see the statue as a symbol of a person God has given them, through sainthood, as a model of faith, but in no way do they worship a statue like an idol or think that it has magic powers. People praying to saints is like divine delegation of responsibility. For instance, when people pray to St. Jude, the patron saint of healing, God is doing the healing. The theory is that the saint has a special relationship with God, and perhaps people could relate to the saint, who is human, better than to God, who is divine.

I've also heard that Catholics think that Mary, the mother of Jesus, is God. Again, that is not the Catholic position. The position is that Mary, as Jesus' mother, has a special relationship with Him, but she in no way is a deity.

When you learn the facts associated with someone's faith, you'll often find that denominations have more in common than you thought. Jesus as the Savior is the essence of Christianity.

Most Christian denominations allow marriages between two people in love who are of different denominations. Sometimes there are restrictions. Some denominations require that a clergy member from both churches cooofficiate at the wedding ceremony. Others specify that children must be raised under the tutelage of one denomination or another. The question remains, How much disagreement is a couple willing to handle?

Decide Which Beliefs You Cannot Accept

If there are certain beliefs you cannot accept, that becomes a personal decision. For instance, the Roman Catholic church believes the sacrament of reconciliation must be done in the presence of a priest, while other denominations hold that reconciliation may be done in private, talking to God.

Decide if Your Relationship Can Survive with
Both Being of Different Denominations

Disagreements on form, as long as you agree on the substance of Christianity, could be solved by a collaborative solution. You'll have to think about the impact of this setup for children. The children could be exposed to both denominations and get the best of both worlds. When they are adults, they could decide to follow one or the other, or they could pick another denomination. The advantage is that they would be tolerant of other faiths, while the disadvantage is that they may be confused by mixed messages. The latter won't be a problem if you, as parents, explain that people see things differently.

The other choice is to have the children follow the denominational beliefs of only one parent. As long as the other parent doesn't feel like that compromises personal beliefs or subjects the children to substantive error, that's fine.

Interfaith Marriages

It's a fact of life that people of different faiths will find each other and fall in love. In many ways, it's the greatest witness one can make. Even Paul says that spouses in interfaith marriage are blessed: "For the unbelieving husband is sanctified by the wife, and the unbelieving wife is sanctified by the husband; otherwise your children would be unclean, but now they are holy" (1 Cor. 7:14).

INFATUATION

The feeling of being in love may start to fade. This can happen for many reasons. One is that infatuation starts to wear off.

Sometimes couples are distressed, believing that there is a big problem in the marriage. Many couples in their twenties call it quits after a few years because infatuation wears off, which is bound to happen as our love's human imperfections cloud our ideal. Other times newness brings infatuation, and that will end with time. It usually takes about four years for infatuation to wear off. (Coincidentally, most couples get married at or near the four-year mark of their relationship.) Sometimes it takes longer. But you can get hit like a ton of bricks when infatuation declines.

> Jessica is a thirty-two-year-old nurse who is gorgeous. She married Ken seven years ago. Ken is an orthopedic surgeon. He is movie-star handsome. Ken is successful, rich, and very nice to everyone he deals with, from patients to nurses to hospital staff to neighbors.
>
> Even after she was married for several years, Jessica's heart would race as she heard Ken come home from work. Her mouth would melt as he kissed her, and her body would ache to be held.
>
> Then one day when Ken came home, Jessica was glad to see him, but she noticed that her heart wasn't pounding. They were still very much in love, but infatuation had worn off, and she was very distressed.

For most couples, infatuation wears off before eight years. But as M. Scott Peck would say, that is the day you really fall in love: the day you see someone as he or she is, faults and all, not as the ideal you created in your mind of the perfect mate. Many couples in their twenties hit the panic button running off to a divorce lawyer at the first hint of marital weariness. Often it's because there are children in the picture, and one partner decides the fun is over with all the responsibilities of being both a parent and a spouse.

Other times, people are used to changing partners every couple of years, and they treat marriage as a dating relationship.

The problem with throwing in the towel when the going gets rough is that no relationship is going to be blissful and satisfying to each person for each day for fifty years or more. Each can love and adore the other for that long, but sometimes the grind of work, endless fighting among kids, illness, suffering, or the money earmarked for new golf clubs having to be spent on braces for the kids' teeth can be disheartening.

These feelings are normal, and they need to be reckoned with. Trading in your spouse for a newer model may or may not be a quick fix (people often find the grass that looked greener from their vantage point was Astroturf!), and it will absolutely create other problems that have to be dealt with.

ADULTERY

Adultery is the darkest of the dark sides of a relationship. Society calls it a fling or an affair, and it is wildly accepted as a victimless crime. (The Bible calls it breaking the seventh commandment [Exod. 20:14].) It's far from victimless, and the victims universally complain of the greatest level of pain ever known when the spouse commits adultery.

Many psychologists explain away adultery saying that it's merely a symptom of a hurting relationship and that the adulterer is, in fact, a victim. Although adultery may be a symptom of a problematic relationship, it's most often selfishness taken to extreme. However, most don't start an adulterous relationship with that intention.

When Jesus was asked if an adulteress should be stoned to death, as was the custom at the time, He said, "He who is without sin among you, let him throw a stone at her first." After everyone had left, Jesus asked the woman if anyone had condemned her. When she replied, "No one, Lord," Jesus said, "Neither do I condemn you; go and sin no more" (John 8:4–11). We need to be careful of the stones we throw at others, no matter whether they are made of granite or castigation.

People often start the adulterous relationship in search of someone to understand them, to agree with them, to appreciate them.

The person with whom they commit adultery may jump at the opportunity to be a friend or a soul mate. The other person may start the relationship as an altruistic sounding board. Other times, they may have a mission from the start and take advantage of someone's vulnerability; they pretend to be caring as a way to get into bed with a desirable partner. It's often simply the thrill of the conquest because a married person is supposedly unavailable.

Married people who commit adultery do so for many reasons.

Reason 1: To Get Even with an Abusive Spouse

Since adultery is the worst act in a long list of horrible things one person can do to another, it's an effective way to make the spouse feel bad without having to confront him or her in any direct way.

Reason 2: To Reestablish Potency

Men and women sometimes are ignored sexually by their spouses. Sometimes it's pure narcissism. A man may suddenly decide that he is too good for his spouse. Even if his spouse is his age, he may want to have sex with someone twice his age or half his age. He wants someone to accept him unconditionally, but he doesn't want to accept his spouse unconditionally.

The four greatest enemies of sexual potency are (1) unresolved conflicts of all types, (2) stress, (3) tiredness, and (4) a busy schedule. Most often when a spouse feels she is being ignored, we find out that the only problem is too many activities or unaddressed problems. Use collaborative problem solving, reduce the stress, get more sleep, and slow life down, and the hormones will start to slosh again. When couples use their extra time to date (see chapter 10), they find their relationship improves and with it so does their sex life.

When couples don't address the sex killers, both partners start to feel bad about themselves, their bodies, and their desirability as sexual beings. These feelings pierce them to the core of their existence. This is what can happen when feelings of being ignored are unaddressed and handled selfishly:

Ralph has been married for fifteen years. He and his wife, Laura, have two children, who are seven and two. Ralph complains that Laura is always a mess, and all she does is lie there once or twice a week when they have sex. He liked it better before they had children; now all she does is nag and complain about being tired.

Clarissa is a receptionist at his workplace. She is twenty-two and vivacious. She always compliments Ralph on his wardrobe. One night on the way out he saw that she was upset, and Clarissa told him that her boyfriend had just called to break up with her.

Ralph called Laura and told her that he had to work late. He took Clarissa to dinner, and they consoled each other. Ralph said that he had been separated (which he wasn't) for nine months. Clarissa was vulnerable and acquiesced to his passes, and they had sex. They continued to rendezvous three or four nights a week.

Ralph thought it was wonderful to be in a relationship with a woman who wasn't constantly complaining about bills or telling him to clean this or take care of that. And she certainly never complained about being tired—he got tired before she did.

Laura, Ralph's wife, is thirty-seven years old. She started dating Ralph when she was in college, and they got married a couple of years later. They tried to have children for several years but couldn't until she started taking fertility drugs.

For the first eight years of their marriage, they had only each other to care about. They would meet after work for spontaneous dinners, and life was carefree. When Caitlin, their daughter, was born, their relationship started changing. Laura's attention had to be split. Now with Anthony, Laura often finds herself torn in many directions.

Laura said, "First of all, I'm still responsible for balancing the checkbook, paying the bills, and taking the kids to day care and picking them up. I have a very stressful job in which I have to deal with irate customers all day. But I earn only a fraction of what the men do.

"Then I get home and have to fix dinner, do laundry, clean the house, and get the kids ready for bed. I even have to mow the lawn.

"What does Ralph do? After I feed the kids, bathe them, referee the constant squabbling, and get them in their pajamas, he reads them a story before bed. Big deal. I'm glad he's doing that, but come on.

"If I ask him to help out, he tells me that he's tired and needs to wind down with a beer. I need to wind down, too, but I've got responsibilities. If he would help out every now and then, maybe I wouldn't be on edge. The last time he romanced me was when we conceived Anthony.

"All I want is a couple of hours of spoiling before we go to bed, like he used to do. 'Oh, honey, you must be so tired after a long day; let me draw a bath for you,' would be nice. What do I get? 'Let's do it.'"

She stopped speaking a moment and then continued. "Even with that trés romantic line, I still make myself find the energy to make love at least once during the week and once on the weekend. I'd be a lot more willing to be more sexy if you noticed me every now and then.

"Gee, we haven't made love in a couple of months because of your 'heavy work schedule.' By the way, when you commit adultery against me, have the decency to use the same type of deodorant. We use Right Guard, and when you come home smelling like Old Spice, it's pretty obvious to me what you're doing."

Laura stormed out of the session and immediately filed for divorce, listing adultery as the grounds.

Clarissa eventually found out that Ralph had lied to her. She said she never would have dated him if she had known, and she broke off the relationship.

Remember, when couples don't make love for a long time (times of stress and extremely heavy schedules, or during or after pregnancy don't count), it's often because conflict is hampering the sex drive. There are therapies for that. Couples can avoid the problems that Ralph and Laura encountered.

222 The Fight-Free Marriage

The search for potency outside marriage is a fool's errand. God will make sure all of your needs are met within marriage.

Reason 3: To Find a Willing Partner Who Doesn't Have to Worry About Life's Realities

Ralph wanted to have his cake and eat it too. He asked much of Laura, and when she did everything he wanted, he forgot that she was human. After working her to the bone physically and emotionally, he didn't do anything to revitalize or assist her in any way. Clarissa didn't put demands on him because dating is about having fun.

Ralph created a lose-lose situation. He wanted more sex, more fun, and a willing wife. Laura certainly got no joy in being over-burdened, and she wanted more fun, more (romantic) sex, and a loving and supportive husband.

Once Ralph crossed the line and committed adultery, the relationship was changed forever. If he could have turned back the hands of time, he would have realized that there were many things he could do to help Laura and ultimately help himself. Instead, he chose to starve, inches from the buffet.

Reason 4: To Pursue an Immoral Lifestyle

Some people, like Ralph, are so self-absorbed that they are willing to hurt their spouses, their children, and anyone else to pursue their pleasures. They fundamentally do not know the difference between right and wrong, and they have difficulty empathizing with those they harm.

Sever the Adulterous Relationship

The past cannot be changed. To preserve a marriage, people who are committing adultery need to sever their adulterous relationship immediately.

Psychologists are divided about the wisdom of confessing the sin to the spouse. Most would agree that spouses know what is going on because of changes in patterns or other signs. Some say adulterers should take this secret to the grave with them. Others say they should confess and ask for mercy—which they usually will not get. Jesus was very clear that He thought that adultery was sufficient reason to divorce. (This must be balanced with Jesus' teaching of forgiveness.)

The psychological toll on being the victim of adultery is astounding. Most crimes of passion—including murder—happen because a spouse cannot forgive or tolerate the idea of the loved one being with another. (Murder is also immoral, and people often spend twenty or so years in jail regretting what they did.) Time heals all wounds, and victims of adultery will find happiness if they trust God and don't take vengeance into their own hands ("Vengeance is Mine, I will repay," says the Lord [Rom: 12:19]).

The saddest part of adultery is that it's always avoidable. If couples work at it, they will find all they need within the covenant of marriage.

HASTY MARRIAGE

Sometimes couples get married hastily and for the wrong reasons (see chapter 9). Even hasty marriages can work, thanks to the covenant with God. The trick is to not view the marriage as a dating relationship and to remember that the rules have changed dramatically.

All the techniques in this book will ease the transition from a dating to a married relationship.

ALCOHOL AND DRUG ABUSE

Alcohol and drug abuse is a big problem. The line between social drinking and alcoholism can be wide or narrow, depending on the person. Many drug addicts swear as they enter court-ordered treatment that their use is only recreational.

Alcohol has physiological properties that affect the body and the mind. Alcohol is a depressant. The feeling of being buzzed or drunk is the body's way of fighting off the depressive effects.

When the nervous system senses alcohol in the body, which it categorizes as a poison (that's where we get the *toxic* in *intoxicated*), it sends signals to pump adrenaline and dopamine into the bloodstream. These hormones fight off the toxins and make the person feel good for a while.

Alcohol is also an anesthetic. Navies used to keep rum on board and have people get so drunk that they could endure or not feel surgery. It's also an emotional anesthetic and can temporarily numb emotional distress.

Alcohol increases sexual desire, which is why couples sometimes report great sex while they were drunk. It also increases aggressiveness, according to Senator Bill Bradley.

The anesthetic effect decreases the senses, which is one reason why bars or a party featuring alcohol seems very loud and why people tend to shout when they are drunk. Their sense of hearing has diminished.

We have built into our brains a center that analyzes behavior and reminds us of the consequences of the behavior. Some people may want to drive fast, for instance, but the fear of being killed or getting a whopper of a speeding ticket modifies their actions. When people drink, the fear of consequences is present, but the alcohol decreases the ability to care about them.

Let's look at the negative effects of alcohol. According to ABC News (*Turning Point* 11/30/94), 18,000 people die in car crashes each year, and 300,000 people are injured when alcohol is involved in a car accident.

We can't know for sure because accurate statistics aren't kept, but we can estimate the following happens when at least one member of the couple is drunk:

- one million conceptions occur
- tens of thousands of people contract HIV, the disease that leads to AIDS
- over one million acts of domestic violence occur

These tragedies get the press. We also have to add to the list everyday cruelty and constant arguing, sapping the lifeblood from marriage. There are also side effects, for example, what happens to Nanette:

Nanette starts getting anxious around two o'clock. She worries about which husband is going to come home. Will she get the nice, nurturing husband, or will he stop at the bar with friends from work and come back mean and aggressive?

By the time she leaves from work, anxiety is at a high. Her stomach gets tight, and all she can think about is, *Am I going to have a nice night, or am I going to have to walk on eggshells?*

This anxiety reaches a peak until he comes home and she knows if he is sober or not.

For Nanette, and many like her, the stress of living with an alcoholic is not only the time when he is drunk but several other hours each day as well.

What to Do

When people drink every day, when they are sober during the week but binge on the weekend, or when they are sober for many months with periods of bingeing, they have a drinking problem. Other signals include feeling unable to make it through a day without alcohol or drugs, needing greater amounts to get the same effect, and damaging familial or work relationships. People who suffer from alcohol abuse are not alone. Thirteen percent of the adult population have had an alcohol abuse problem at some time in their lives.[3]

If people have any of the symptoms listed above, they need to talk to their doctor, a pastor, a trusted friend, or AA (Alcoholics Anonymous) and see if they have a problem. Maybe they don't. If they do, the doctor, AA, or others can recommend help for them so they can begin living happy lives again.

If you are living with someone who is an alcoholic, you need to talk to someone from AA or Al-Anon. Both groups are experienced in helping people who live with alcoholic spouses or parents.

One general strategy is that conflict resolution should wait until the person is sober, if at all possible. Dealing with someone at the height of aggressiveness will distort the situation and complicate the collaborative process.

Don't Wait until Rock Bottom

Many people with an alcohol or drug problem wait until they've hit rock bottom to seek help. The bubble of denial that nothing is wrong continues until they've lost their checking accounts, their jobs, their houses, and possibly their families. They may also have had their freedom taken away by being put in jail.

People who are wise contact their doctor or AA long before their problems get out of hand. If you know any of the millions of people who could use help, don't hesitate to suggest to them it's never too late to start.

WHEN RELATIONSHIPS GO SOUTH

If your relationship goes south, remember that most of the time solutions can be found that will be good for everyone. Communicating your concerns as soon as you can makes the collaboration process easiest. You can repair your relationships one small step at a time.

Final Thoughts

CHAPTER TWELVE

Now that you know details of *The Fight-Free Marriage,* here are some final words.

GIVE THINGS TIME

Some parts of Conflict Without Casualty will hit you like a bolt of lightning. Aspects of personality type like the Introvert/ Extrovert preference are immediately noticeable. But conflict resolution is different. Learning how to do that can take a while.

Since conflict resolution style is learned, we may have been relying on avoiding or taking control for many years. Learning collaboration is the goal, but like going into cold water, most of us will ease into it.

People who are conflict avoiders need to assure themselves that important relationships won't be damaged or destroyed by collaborative problem solving, and in fact, just the opposite is true. They start conflict resolution on small issues, and as they get more and more confident, they start tackling the larger ones.

Those who have a hard conflict resolution style are wary about collaboration because they are afraid of losing control. They gain confidence when they let others make decisions and they see that the sky doesn't fall in. Relieving some responsibility can be freeing for the person with the hard style as well as the spouse and children. Again, this is accomplished little by little.

In any case, give yourself at least a couple of months.

WHAT MAKES US HAPPY

Jonathan Freedman in his book *Happy People*[1] surveyed a hundred thousand people on various aspects of their lives that made them happy. Here are the results:

Rank	Single Men	Single Women
1	Friends and social life	Friends and social life
2	Job or primary activity	Being in love
3	Being in love	Job or primary activity
4	Recognition, success	Recognition, success
5	Sex life	Personal growth
6	Personal growth	Sex life
7	Finances	Health
8	House or apartment	Body and attractiveness
9	Body and attractiveness	Finances
10	Health	House or apartment

Rank	Married Men	Married Women
1	Personal/spiritual growth	Being in love
2	Being in love	Marriage
3	Marriage	Partner's happiness
4	Job or primary activity	Sex life
5	Partner's happiness	Recognition, success
6	Sex life	Personal, spiritual growth
7	Recognition, success	Job or primary activity
8	Friends and social life	Friends and social life
9	Being a parent	Health
10	Finances	Being a parent

Once people are married, some develop grievances against their spouses. If you or someone you know has these grievances, you'll find strategies for dealing with them in this book.

THE TOP TEN MOST SERIOUS GRIEVANCES OF SOME MARRIED PEOPLE

Rank	Complaints Husbands Have About Wives	Complaints Wives Have About Husbands
1	Nags me	Selfish and inconsiderate
2	Unaffectionate	Unsuccessful in business

Rank	Complaints Husbands Have About Wives	Complaints Wives Have About Husbands
3	Selfish and inconsiderate	Untruthful
4	Complains too much	Complains too much
5	Interferes with my hobbies	Doesn't show affection
6	Slovenly in appearance	Doesn't talk things over
7	Quick tempered	Harsh with children
8	Interferes with discipline	Touchy
9	Conceited	Not interested in children
10	Insincere	Not interested in home

Based on what we know about conflict styles and personality type, it's no wonder why couples have these grievances. Most of the time, the grievances result from misperceptions or misunderstandings or underdeveloped or inadequate conflict resolution skills.

The good news is that after reading this book, you are now armed with the information you need to clear up any concerns that you or your spouse may have.

IF YOU'RE ENGAGED

Engagement time is a transition. As you make the transition into your new life together, remember that a wedding is a day, and a marriage is a lifetime. Couples who keep that in perspective and put the proportional amount of time and effort into what's important find that married life is easier.

With that being said, your wedding day does need to be special to you as a couple and to the people who are important to you. Do all you can to make sure that it's special for everyone.

Enjoy your honeymoon and your new life together.

TAPE YOUR VOWS

If you have a videotape of your vows, watch it every anniversary and maybe once during the year too. If you ever have doubts about what your spouse thinks about you, it's summed up there.

If you've been married a while, you probably don't have a tape because video cameras weren't common a few years ago. Today, if you don't have a camera, borrow someone's. If you can't do that, you can rent one for under twenty dollars at most video stores.

If you don't have a tape, remember what was said or look to your church's standard vows.

REMEMBER GOD IS IN YOUR CORNER

God can sustain your joy and help you through the tough times. You'll have both because that's the nature of human relations. Sometimes we get so caught up in the nadirs and the zeniths of life that we forget God is there for us. It's never too late.

IF YOU'VE CAUGHT THE BUS, KEEP RUNNING

When I wrote *Personality Selling,* I advised salespeople that after they caught the bus (made the sale), they should stop running (quit talking).

For couples, my advice is the opposite. After you've caught the bus, *keep* running. Treat your spouse with the same vim and vigor as when you met. People never take their new love for granted—so keep running and your spouse will always feel special.

New couples touch once every seven seconds and kiss over one hundred times a day. Married couples touch less than once an hour and kiss only four times a day. Up the average. It can only help. And so your spouse doesn't have to worry about being loved, say it each day any way you can.

YOU DON'T HAVE TWO JOBS

Marriage isn't a second job that you don't get paid for. If you understand yourself and your spouse and you can resolve conflicts so that everyone wins, you'll come home from your job and have a vacation waiting for you.

ONE FINAL THOUGHT

I hope what I have written will help your love and your relationship be all that they can be and they will constantly grow deeper and more wonderful. Let me finish this book with a line from the hit musical *Les Misérables:*

> To love another person
> Is to see the face of God.

Conflict Resolution
in
Abusive Relationships

Including a section on abusive relationships in a book about relationships that are designed to last forever may seem odd. Although I believe in the sanctity of marriage, and I strongly believe that marriage vows are sacred, I don't want people to stay in a relationship that ultimately will get them seriously harmed or even killed.

The subject of abusive relationships is a sensitive one. Where does one draw the line? Answers to your personal situation cannot be found in this or any book. This is a subject to talk to a counselor or a minister or a priest about. A goal is to stay together for life; however, you never have to put yourself or your children in harm's way.

It seems to me that if the marriage vows are clearly broken, one can end the relationship. Abusive behavior is cowardly and does not love, honor, or cherish a spouse.

Many times people find that the relationship can improve once serious and drastic steps to halt the violence have begun. Keeping an abusive relationship going doesn't work because the relationship is doomed to end anyway. Even if the victim is totally compliant, the abuser will end up in jail or kill the victim. The sooner action is taken, the better.

MOST SPOUSES ARE NOT VIOLENT

Most spouses are not violent or abusive to their mates or to their children. Nevertheless 50 percent of all women who are murdered are killed by their male partners. Men, too, are the victims of abuse, but they are unwilling to share their experience or report the abuse. People are not doing God's work by being a punching bag or a shooting range target.

CHRISTIANITY IS NOT A LICENSE TO ABUSE

Therapists often say that certain violent or abusive Christians are the most difficult to heal. This is a shame because Jesus was never violent, and those who hurt others in His name are doing a disservice to their families and to their God.

God does not want us to harm our families either sexually or physically. God is often used as an excuse for people hurting others. They have a script that goes like this: they turn to the Bible to justify their abuse; then I'm supposed to refute their beliefs, and they greet me with another Bible verse.

This attitude flies in the face of Jesus, who wanted us to love each other. Sometimes they'll convince themselves that their abuse is tough love. Abuse is not love. Breaking the bubble of denial that is around them can be difficult. Even when these people are put in jail for murdering a child or a spouse, they insist that they are doing God's work. My wish for them is that they seek help before it's too late.

Invariably, they have believed incorrectly all their lives that God wants them to be abusive, and they may have been victims of abuse. If they ever saw the fallout of their abuse on their children or their spouses, even twenty years later, they would realize how awful they had been.

THEY WOULDN'T TURN THE TIDE

Abusive people may use discipline as an excuse for being abusive.

People Have Other Events in Their Lives

When people have a conflict in their lives that they don't address, they may take it out on an innocent party. This is called *displacement*. If someone's boss is horrible to him and the conflict is not addressed, when that person gets home, he may beat up his child or spouse since he cannot beat up his boss.

Displacement is very hard to pick up on because the originating event may not be clear. Abuse masked as discipline is especially horrifying to the innocent victim.

People Take Advantage of Their Physical Size

A mean part of me would love to have an NFL linebacker around when I hear people say that hitting hard enough to cause bruises or bleeding is good for kids in the long run. Most abusers take advantage of their size, thinking they are impervious to harm. I'd like to have a three-hundred-pound linebacker on hand because I know they would change their tune if every time they spilled their water, were late, or didn't pay a bill, they got knocked around in the very same manner they do their families.

As logical as my fantasy sounds, the persecutors need to heal their own pain and learn appropriate ways to cope. Threats of violence or extended jail time may decrease the behavior but not solve the problem.

Sexual Abuse Is Not Education

Child molesters often convince themselves their abuse is justified because it is sex education. It is not education, and it continues to hurt children many years after the abuse occurred.

ABUSERS NEED TO TAKE ACTION

People who are being abused need to take action. Abusers, whether sexual or physical, must also immediately take action to stop their behavior. As cowardly as being abusive is, it is equally courageous to begin the steps to stop hurting others. We know that abusers were often victims themselves, so they have to deal with hurting others they love as well as being hurt themselves. It's not easy, but it's worth it. Denial that abuse is happening or has occurred is a common problem. Minimizing the impact of abuse on others and blaming others or situations are symptoms of the problem. *Abusers cannot change the past, but they can change the future.*

A PSYCHOLOGY OF ABUSE

The psychology of abuse has three parts: (1) the cycle of violence, (2) conflict resolution style, and (3) learned helplessness.

The Cycle of Violence

The cycle of violence is predictable. Part of its scariness is its predictability. Here are the four stages[1]:

2. The Attack

1. The Tension Buildup   3. The Honeymoon Period

4. Denial, Minimization, and Blame

Stage 1: The tension buildup. Tension runs high. Victims walk on eggshells. If the cycle of violence has been repeated a few times, the victim knows that an attack is imminent. She is scared and lives in fear of saying or doing the wrong thing. She tends to avoid conflict at all costs, though occasionally she will provoke a conflict so the attack will occur and she won't have to be in suspense of when it's going to happen.

> Jessica's husband, Neil, worked as a personnel manager at a bank. Every time the quarterly reviews had to be done, he would be overworked and distraught. Jessica knew that if she made the slightest criticism or comment, Neil would fly off the handle.
> She knew the situation was worse when he didn't get sleep, which he wasn't doing. She would give in to all of his demands, economic, sexual, and everything else. Jessica was terrified of saying or doing something that would upset him.

Stage 2: The attack. After the tension buildup, the attack occurs. It can be a punch, a slap, or a push, or weapons can be used. Sometimes the victim is choked or even raped. There are many types of attacks, but they all have one element in common: the attacker is controlling and hurting the victim.

> Neil asked Jessica to make love. Though she didn't really want to, she acquiesced so as not to anger him. He ejaculated almost immediately, which she didn't know. When he asked her if she had an orgasm, she told him, "Not yet."

Furious, he called her frigid and got out of bed. When she asked him in her most seductive tone to come back to bed and try again, he punched her in the jaw. (In the police report, he said that he wanted her to shut up.)

Stage 3: The honeymoon period. In the honeymoon period, the attacker is very nice to the victim. The attacker will wine and dine the spouse and be charming and wonderful. The attack will not be mentioned, or if it is, it will be talked about only as "the incident" or "what happened."

The honeymoon may last for an afternoon or a month or even a year, though the honeymoon tends to get shorter and shorter with each pass through the cycle.

After Jessica got back from the hospital, Neil told her how sorry he was. He would get help, and it would never happen again. He told her not to leave him and said how much he loved her. To show his sincerity, he became the model husband in her eyes and treated her much the same as when they were dating.

Jessica liked the honeymoon period so much that she believed him, though a voice inside her sounded a warning.

Stage 4: Denial, minimization, and blame. After the honeymoon period is over, denial, minimization, and blame take over, or DMB as psychologists call it. Both the victim and the abuser participate. The victim says things like, "If I hadn't been so insensitive," or "I should have known he was upset," or "I asked for it," or "It wasn't such a big deal," or "It was my fault."

The abuser will agree or say things like, "I just pushed her," or "She fell the wrong way," or "She made a big deal out of nothing." Other times he will not admit the event happened.

Back to Stage 1: Then the tension builds up, and the victim again walks on eggshells anticipating the next attack.

People need to realize that there is a cycle and that it won't be broken on its own.

After Neil broke Jessica's jaw and it had to be wired shut, he was put in jail for a week and ordered to do two hundred hours of community service work at a soup kitchen frequented by battered women. Finally, he understood he had a problem. He went to counseling. In the two years since he has been in counseling, he hasn't been abusive.

When Neil feels tense, he tells Jessica, and they realize that his problems at work are their problems as a couple and they work on them together.

One time he got the urge to strike out at Jessica, but he realized that (1) he would go to jail for six months since he was on probation, (2) hitting her wouldn't solve anything, and (3) he had a moral responsibility to love, honor, and cherish her.

Instead of hitting her, he focused on his feelings: "I am so angry with my boss for making me work eighty hours a week." Jessica could be supportive rather than frightened, fearing that she was going to be hit.

There is a lot more to solving the violence problem than what Neil did. Working through this issue takes months, not minutes. If you are a victim or an abuser, look in the phone book for free referrals. There is only honor in seeking help.

The second aspect of the psychology of abuse is the conflict resolution style taken to the limit.

Conflict Resolution Style and Abuse

Janine had a yield-lose style. Her husband, Lionel, would get drunk and be verbally abusive to her. Sometimes he would hit her. After he hit her, he would leave the house and then feel bad. He would be nice to her for a couple of weeks. Then the cycle would start again. Because Janine was in the yield-lose style, she yielded to the beating; she knew the attack phase would end and the honeymoon phase would begin, even though she would lose by feeling degraded and being injured.

Psychologists, psychiatrists, and social workers know that spousal abuse gets worse and worse and that as people yield to one level of abuse, the abusers will keep pushing the envelope until they are cured from their problem or they end up in jail.

If you find yourself in the yield-lose style taken to the extreme, or you are taking advantage of someone in this mode and it has led to violence, get help for yourself immediately.

The lose-lose style taken to its extreme can lead to dire consequences. If people are tired of losing, or they just don't see that they'll ever win, they can become violent or desperate without regard to the consequences. They may kill or hurt someone and not care if they will go to jail. That is not a good situation, and it's one that people will regret once they're out of that mode—but it's often too late.

If people you know are in such an extreme lose-lose mode that they are willing to commit an act of violence, tell the police or find a state agency. There is help for these people, who often are good, but desperate people lacking knowledge of healthy ways to resolve conflicts.

Learned Helplessness

The psychological term for a soft style in the face of violence is *learned helplessness,* which Nazi Germany knew a lot about and used to its advantage. Learned helplessness is debilitating. People experiencing this effect see no way out of their predicament, so they just allow the abuse to go on and give up trying to find answers. Some psychologists believe that people don't want to use up energy defending themselves because they see that as wasted effort.

If you or anyone you know has given up, it is like a boxer in the corner with his hands over his face allowing someone to pummel him at will. Immediately advise such a person to go to the police, a shelter, a psychologist, or a minister. These people are experienced in dealing with people who are suffering from learned helplessness.

Taking yourself out of harm's way is not an unchristian, unbecoming, or weak action. If you're experiencing learned helplessness, one symptom is feeling that making a call for help will accomplish nothing. It's a local call and can be confidential. There is nothing to lose and a tremendous amount to gain. Don't fool yourself into thinking things will get better on their own—they won't. Any police officer will tell you that people who are abusive will stop that type of behavior only when they get therapy or end up in jail, and jail is the usual stop. The problem is that as the abuse gets worse, the victim feels that nothing can be done.

That's the expected response, but believe in the wisdom of seeking help. You're breaking the cycle.

Almost always abusive people hate that part of who they are. They're searching for help too. Chances are that they were victims at one time, and they have a burning desire they don't understand to hurt others. These people are always grateful that they stop being abusive, and they often lament that they have to hurt people they love or face serious social consequences, like prison, before they change their ways.

If you feel uncomfortable about helping yourself or someone you love who is experiencing learned helplessness, know that you are doing God's work by helping both parties.

LEFTOVERS

A person's life doesn't begin at marriage. Each spouse has eighteen or more years of living prior to the union. That's a lot of miles. In that time, much happened that can affect any relationship. I refer to these problems as leftovers.

Child Abuse

This is the most common and one of the most serious leftovers. Hundreds of thousands of boys and girls have reported being sexually or physically abused by the time they are eighteen.

People assume that since they were abused long ago, the problem is over. Sometimes it is, and sometimes it isn't—and usually it isn't.

Adults who were victims of child abuse often have trouble in intimate relationships. They often feel shame or embarrassment at what happened. The good news is that we have therapies that we know can work to help you. If you don't have the money for a therapist in private practice, you can get therapy through government-sponsored agencies.

It's important to get help because your spouse and/or your

children can be victims of the terrible things that happened to you. Here's how.

You enter another abusive relationship. When people are abused, they may enter other abusive relationships. They may have talked themselves into thinking they're not worthy of a loving relationship. Or the spouse may take the place of the abuser, and the abused person wants to tell the spouse off in place of the abuser.

This is a very strong urge. Many battered women return to their batterers as the cycle of violence perpetuates. The cycle is broken only when the batterer ends up incarcerated or the battered woman dies. Sometimes she gets out of the relationship, but only when she can convince herself that she doesn't deserve to be harmed.

Upon seeing a woman in his courtroom for the third time seeking a restraining order, a judge told her, "I keep on giving restraining orders, and you keep going back and end up in the emergency room. I can only surmise that you like getting beat up." She didn't like being a victim; she just didn't know how to end the cycle. She went back home and was bludgeoned to death.

You can repeat the behavior with your children. Child-abuse victims generally fall into two categories: (1) those who continue to do the horrible things done to them and (2) those who vow never to violate a child. If you are a victim of child abuse and have children, you must have it clear in your mind that you will not lash out at your own children.

Effective therapies can help you resolve childhood pains without resorting to inflicting pain on your own offspring.

YOU NEVER HAVE TO PUT YOURSELF IN HARM'S WAY

You never, never have to put yourself in harm's way. If you are in danger or if you are receiving physical or emotional abuse, you *do not* have a moral responsibility to endure it.

You always have the right to protect yourself. Talk to your minister or consult the police or phone book about where to find shelters. If necessary, get temporary restraining orders.

An abusive spouse is not loving, honoring, and cherishing you, which is a breach of the marriage vows. You must seek safety.

You may be able to keep your marriage vows, or you may decide that you cannot restore a loving and trusting relationship. But if you separate from the abusive partner, make it clear that you are doing so only temporarily until the abuse stops, and that you wish to invent options that allow you to maintain your relationship.

NOTES

Chapter 1

1. M. Scott Peck, *The Road Less Traveled* (New York: Touchstone Books, 1978).
2. Abigail Van Buren, *Dear Abby on Planning Your Wedding* (New York: Andrews and McMeel, 1988).
3. Carl Jung, *Psychological Types* (New York: Harcourt Press, 1923).
4. The Myers-Briggs Type Indicator is a registered trademark of Consulting Psychologists Press, Palo Alto, California. The MBTI is a trademark of Consulting Psychologists Press, Palo Alto, California.
5. Thomas More, "Personality Tests are Back," *Fortune,* March 1987, 72–84.

Chapter 2

1. Robert Benfari, *Understanding Your Management Style* (New York: Free Press, 1991).
2. Roger Fisher and William Ury, *Getting to Yes: Negotiating Agreements Without Giving In* (New York: Houghton Mifflin, 1981),· 101.

Chapter 3

1. A guide to the use and development of the Myers-Briggs Type Indicator (Palo Alto, Calif.: Consulting Psychologists Press, 1985).
2. Ibid.
3. David Keirsey and Marilyn Bates, *Please Understand Me: Character and Temperament Type* (Del Mar, Calif: Prometheus Nemesis Books, 1978), 14.
4. Ibid.
5. Mary Chase, *Harvey* (New York: Dramatists Play Service, 1943).

Chapter 5

1. Personality Selling® is a registered trademark of Sales and Negotiation Training Company.
2. Robert M. Bramson, *Coping with Difficult People* (New York: Dell, 1988).

Chapter 9

1. Harry Stack Sullivan, ed., *The Interpersonal Theory of Psychiatry* (New York: Norton, 1968).

Chapter 10

1. William Masters and Virginia Johnson, *Masters and Johnson on Sex and Human Loving.*

Chapter 11

1. Charles W. Price, *Life after Bankruptcy* (Tallahassee: Practical Publications, 1993).
2. This comes from a multidisciplinary document called BEM in which church leaders from a variety of denominations got together to see what areas of agreement there were among denominations.
3. *Diagnostic and Statistical Manual of Mental Disorders,* 3rd edition-revised, American Psychiatric Association 1987 (Washington, DC: American Psychiatric).

Chapter 12

1. Jonathan Freedman, *Happy People* (New York: Harcourt Brace Jovanovich, 1978).

Appendix

1. Lee Ann Hoys, *Battered Women As Survivors* (New York: Rutledge, 1990).

About the Author

Tom Anastasi is a practicing therapist in New Hampshire who specializes in marital and premarital counseling. Educated at Harvard University, he also teaches Negotiation and Organizational Behavior at Boston University's School of Management. As director of Sales and Negotiation Training Company, he travels around the country doing motivational speeches and conducting seminars on the practical uses of psychology in negotiation and conflict resolution. Tom lives in Nashua, New Hampshire, with his wife, Donna, and his daughter, Amy, and attends Faith Episcopal Church in Merrimack, New Hampshire.